**THE TIMES TRAVEL LIBRARY**

Edited by Paul Zach

Times Editions
422 Thomson Road, Singapore 1129
© Copyright by Times Editions, 1988

Printed by Tien Wah Press, Singapore
Color separated by Colourscan, Singapore
Typeset by Superskill Graphics, Singapore

**Cover:** A procession of Yi clan elders honors the kings and
queens of the former Yi Dynasty at Chong-myo, the Royal
Ancestral Shrine. This solemn but colorful rite is held on the
first Sunday of May each year.
**Endpapers:** Jubilant South Korean athletes swarm onto the
Olympic Stadium field during the grand finale of the 1986
Asian Games — the staging of the games served as a
successful trial run for the 1988 Olympics.
**Frontispiece:** South Korea plays China in the men's
badminton finals during the 1986 Asian Games at Seoul's
new Olympic Sports. Such international sports events have
helped speed Seoul's rapid rise to worldwide prominence.

Publisher's number: 417
ISBN: 9971-40-127-4

# SEOUL

Photographs by George Mitchell
Text by Rose E. Lee

Designed by Leonard Lueras

First Edition 1988

TIMES EDITIONS

**This page:** *The landmark Nam-san, or Seoul Tower, at dusk, is a popular observation point for panoramic views of South Korea's capital.*

**Following pages:** *Koreans from all parts of the country come to Seoul in search of bargains and at the sprawling Namdae-mun Market shoppers mill around under a sign which warns: "Fire, Fire, Fire. Beware of Fire!"; a young family and two coeds descend Mt. Nam-san after a fun-filled excursion to the large public park on its slopes; the city's ever-widening streets force pedestrians to take the high road during the evening rush hour; and, lights in Seoul's skyscrapers burn late, as this scene from the residential hills north of the city reveals, because office workers regularly put in ten to twelve hours days.*

# Contents

# Seoul

## *The Center of Everything*

**B**efore the night sky brightens to a dull gray in the early morning hours, before the basso rumble of city buses begins to compete with the honk of taxi drivers darting from lane to lane, another sound greets the new day. It is the rhythmic stomp of boots on the pavement as dozens of young draftees run in unison behind a drill master down Seoul's main thoroughfare, Chong-no, chanting and singing.

The somber discipline is a marked contrast to the sheer chaos that soon follows as morning commuters engage in a mad free-for-all to get to work or school. As even the simple start to the morning in Seoul reveals, South Koreans possess an instinct for rigid restraint and unflagging vigilance even as they exhibit an innate individualism and aggressive energy.

At first these two traits may appear to be contradictory, but there is a unifying thread — the intense, single-minded determination with which Koreans approach everything they do. And this double-barreled dose of discipline and determination has produced one of Asia's great modern cities. Seoul is not just great in the literal sense — its population is approaching ten million — but in the classic sense as well. It rose miraculously from the ashes of the Korean War: only a generation later, the sprawl of ramshackle houses and shops that look like they were tacked together from U.S. Army-surplus material is rapidly giving way to the tall monuments of steel, glass and concrete that signify economic success.

First-time visitors, whose image of Korea has been shaped by a weird blend of episodes from the television comedy M*A*S*H and news clips of rioting students, are always amazed to find Seoul a human settlement of such magnitude and modernity. Even long-time residents of the city who leave for just a few months are startled when they return to find painters and landscapers putting the finishing touches on skyscrapers that have sprouted from what had been huge pits in the ground. Neighborhoods have been razed, new apartment blocks opened, roads, bridges, and tunnels built; the roads are filled with gleaming new models of locally-made cars, the same ones that are starting to be seen on roads in Europe and the United States.

The rapid change is the product of one of the world's fastest growing economies. Fortunately, though, in its frenzied rush to the

future the city has not left behind all of the cultural and historical riches of its past. Seoul still has a timeless quality about it.

Part of that is due to the lie of the land. Steep slopes covered with young trees and scrub that surround the sheer granite cliffs overlooking the city rise to the north, west and east of South Korea's government district. In 1950, during the Korean War, the hills on the north and west were the scene of intense trench warfare and fierce hand-to-hand combat. General Douglas MacArthur's troops streamed in from a daring landing at Inch'ŏn to retake Seoul from the North Koreans.

*Schoolgirls show off the traditional Korean costume, the* hanbok, *during the colorful closing ceremonies of the 1986 Asian Games (left) while two schoolboys heading home (above) wait to board Seoul's modern answer to the school bus, the subway.*

15

Today the mountains are still the preserve of the Korean army. One unexpected benefit of the military presence has been the preservation of a large patch of greenery in a city where the crush of humanity would otherwise have obliterated every natural open space years ago.

In fact, in the spring the bloom of yellow forsythia and purple azalea, closely followed by white magnolia and pink cherry blos-

soms, belies the ugly fact that South Korea is still a nation technically at war. On weekends and holidays at this time of year, thousands of Koreans hike north up to the stretch of mountains in this sensitive military perimeter. Families and friends stake out small plots next to trickling mountain streams where they barbecue strips of marinated beef and pork and wash down the tasty morsels with beer or *soju*, a potent grain liquor. They sing and dance and listen to the sound of their own bellowing voices echo off distant peaks.

In yet another jarring, revealing contrast, Koreans work with unparalleled ferocity.

*Namdae-mun, the Great South Gate, stands out as an enduring symbol of Seoul's great heritage even though it is surrounded by traffic and highrises (left). Nearby, a delivery boy pedals past a giant rendition of the Asian Games symbol (above).*

17

And they play with an equally-intense abandon that seems to controvert the very meaning of the word leisure.

Seoul is the center of Korea. "We thought it was the center of the world," says a Korean professor who has emigrated to the United States but still longs for the tension and sense of purpose that marked his days as a student in Seoul. He and his classmates, now his friends for life, had is largely filled with families who abandoned their farm homes after generations of tilling the soil. They pile into low-rise houses separated by narrow winding lanes that climb over the rolling hills of the city. There, they live sometimes three or four to a room, hoping a son will pass the lottery of national educational tests and help lift the family from poverty.

Of course, it's not a lottery per se: chance

marched in the streets in an attempt to bring democracy to South Korea; they had debated at length profound issues like social justice and political freedom in dingy little cafes outside the university gates.

The issues — and the political villains and heroes — have changed since then, but the cafes are still there and Korean boys continue to make the transition from adolescence to manhood by singing over round-after-round of milky white *makkŏlli*, a tangy fermented rice wine priced for the wallets of improverished students.

Many of the students are children of migrants from the countryside. Seoul today

*The Myŏng-dong alleyways (right) thrive in the early evening as office workers squeeze in some last-minute shopping before heading home. Coveted items include imported designer fashions, like these shoes in a high-tech display (above).*

plays little part in the outcome. Korean children slave over their books in hopes of scoring well enough to enter one of the country's leading educational institutions, particularly Seoul National University. It's a ticket, though not an automatic one, into the Korean elite.

Seoul has been the seat of that elite, the center of political power and culture in a richly-diverse rural society, for almost 600 years. Unlike the unrestrained, haphazard growth of modern Seoul, the founding of the city was carefully conceived.

According to ancient Chinese geomantic traditions, the site where Seoul is located was perfect for a capital: the protective mountain ridges, or "bones," on the north, east and west repel evil, while life-sustaining rivers, the "blood," flow on its east, west and southern flanks.

The first hint that the area might spawn a great city came in a prophecy revealed to the founder of the Koryŏ Dynasty in AD 918. It predicted Seoul would become the dynastic capital of the Yi family. In an attempt to prevent that from happening, the Koryŏ king planted plum trees on the slopes of Pugak Mountain in Seoul; the Chinese character for Yi means "plum." Later the trees were shorn down and the roots yanked

Mountain is the Blue House, South Korea's Presidential Mansion and executive offices.

The semi-circle of tall mountains provided an excellent natural defense against invasion from the north, the principal fear of the founders of the Yi Dynasty. Ironically, it turned out to be invaders from the south, the Japanese, who plagued the dynasty and eventually triggered its collapse in 1910 when they seized the peninsula.

up in a symbolic attempt to defeat a potential rival ruling family.

The effort proved a colossal failure. When Yi Tae-jo founded his Chosŏn Dynasty, also known as the Yi Dynasty, in 1392, he called on his old friend, the monk Muhak — literally "ignorant" or "without learning" in Korean — who selected the spot at the base of Pugak Mountain.

The remains of Yi's palace, the Kyŏngbok-kung, still stands on the original site along with the new National Museum, which was installed in the former Capitol Building erected by the Japanese. Behind the old palace on the lower slopes of Pugak

Although Yi Tae-jo was responsible for choosing the city's site, it was King Sejong who was the primary impetus in the building of Seoul. His influence on its present shape is still evident. He rebuilt the city walls that had been hastily erected by Yi Tae-jo, strengthening Seoul's defenses. Only recently repaired in the 1970s by the late President Park Chung-hee, the walls that snake over the top of Pugak Mountain look like a scaled-down version of the Great Wall of China. What they lack in immensity, they make up for in charm.

The city walls and the enormous gates, which have also been restored and designated "national treasures," once physically defined the perimeters of Seoul, or Hansŏng-bu as it was known during most of the Yi Dynasty. All of the great Korean universities are concentrated inside the

*Clowning schoolchildren are as common a sight in Seoul as they are in other countries. This engaging group of hardy youngsters (above) are bundled up in the kind of sporty western-style garments that South Korea exports to the world.*

borders of the capital as is all of the country's cultural and artistic life. More than 90 per cent of all Korean companies are registered in Seoul, because it is where nearly all business occurs.

Not only has Seoul become the epicenter of Korean life, it has grown into a city of increasing international importance that boasts more than 50 foreign bank branches. Foreign manufacturing companies have

also been rushing in to take advantage of South Korea's rapid mastery of new technologies. Inevitably these newcomers have helped make Seoul truly cosmopolitan.

Namsan, which means "South Mountain," once marked the southern boundary of the city but, with its tall television transmission and observation tower, it is now a rather obvious central point. Seoul began spreading south of the Han River at the start of the Korean War. On June 25, 1950, hundreds of thousands of residents streamed over the single bridge that spanned the Han River. Some waited for days before they could cross. However, it wasn't until the construction of modern Yŏ'ui-do, that the city began spreading south of the river in earnest. Today, more than 50 per cent of the population commutes back and forth over

the 16 car and rail bridges that have been built over the Han; there is more population concentrated south of the river than north of it.

South of the river, or Kang-nam, the streets run straight and meet at right angles and form tidy squares that enclose row after row of tall apartment and office blocks. From the air they look like toy matchbox models run amok.

These modern apartments are devoid of

the character of older thatched or tile-roofed features of Korean architecture, but they have meant a vast improvement in the quality of housing for many Koreans. The highrises also lack the all-important patch of ground where Koreans bury the family crock of *kimch'i*, the fiery-hot, garlicky, pickled vegetables that are an essential component of the national diet. This fermented delicacy (which the uninitiated may find to be an indelicacy) loses its beloved flavor when frozen on the apartment balcony during the winter. For the affluent, modern technology has found a solution to the problem — the *kimch'i* refrigerator.

*During Seoul's long hard winter, temperatures often plunge far below freezing point. At such times, South Koreans almost disappear under layers of clothing. Here above, a bespectacled elder fights the cold with a proper old-fashioned hat and thick muffler.*

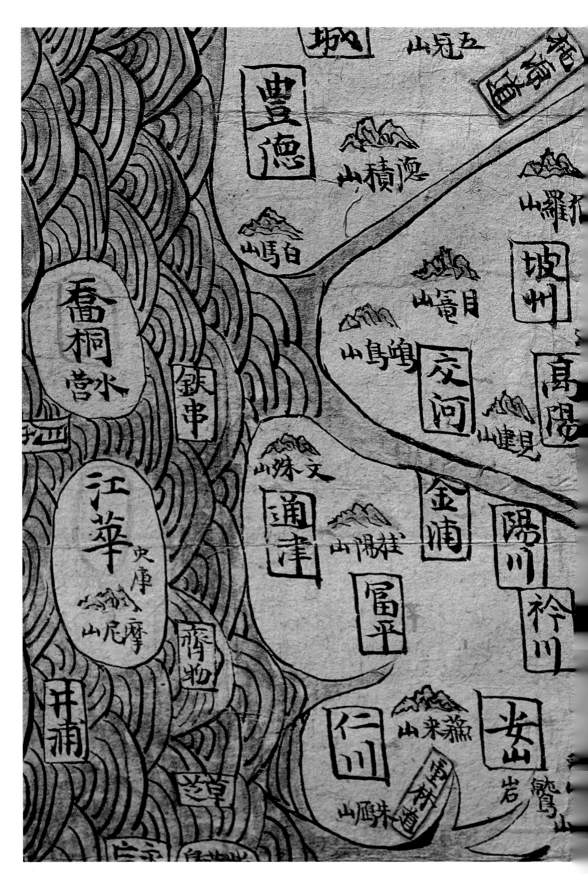

永平

積城

山岳紺

山留道

抱川

海龍山

加平

山岳花

山舩三

山岩佛

楊州

山宝天

山岳雲

山白

京都

道丘平

山積沙

山遊馬

山門龍

楊根

山嶽

江漢

山寬木

良才道

山溪清

利平

又有竹杖庵

有李檣大藏

經記

果川

廣州

山明黙

有露翠津

龍仁

慶安道

山龜南

山京圓

山城北

23

# Historical Chronology

**4000-3000 BC** — First human settlements occur in the Seoul area during the Neolithic Period.

**700-20 BC** — Bronze Age implements found north and south of the Han River are believed to date to this period.

**18 AD** — The Kingdom of Paekche establishes a capital in the Han River valley in the present area of Seoul greater metropolitan.

**AD 757** — The Seoul area is named Hanyang-gun under the powerful Shilla Kingdom.

**1067** — The Koryŏ king Munjong builds a summer palace on the slopes of Inwang-san, on the west side of the city. He renames the area Namgyŏng, the "Southern Capital."

**1308** — The name of the capital is changed again, to Hanyang-bu.

**1394** — Hanyang-bu becomes the capital of the newly-founded Yi Dynasty under the dynastic founder Yi Tae-jo. He calls the city Hansŏng-bu.

**1395** — Construction of the Kyŏngbok Palace and six government ministries is completed. Fortified earthen ramparts are built around the perimeter of the city.

**1396** — King T'aejo finishes construction of the four great and four lesser gates of the city. Several are still standing but have undergone extensive rebuilding and restoration several times over the years.

**1403** — Chong-no becomes the city's commercial center and remains so until the 1960s.

**1404** — The first census of the Yi Dynasty finds that the population of Hansŏng-bu has reached 100,000.

**1405** — Construction of the Ch'angdŏk Palace is completed.

**1406** — The Tŏksu Palace is completed.

**1422** — King Sejong, one of the greatest rulers in Korean history, rebuilds the city walls with stone.

**1443** — Han'gŭl, a phonetic writing system for the Korean language, is promulgated after being developed by a team of scholars under the personal direction of King Sejong.

**1592** — The Hideyoshi invasions from Japan begin and continue for the next six years. They result in major destruction in the capital. During the disorder, Korean slaves burn the Kyŏngbok Palace to the ground. The war produces an important Korean hero, Admiral Yi Sun-sin, who invents the world's first armor-clad ship.

**1636** — The Manchus of China's Ch'ing Dynasty sweep through the Korean peninsula and wreak havoc and destruction in Hansŏng-bu. The Yi Dynas-

STONE DOG, GUARDIAN OF PALACE AGAINST FIRE

*Vintage photographs of Seoul's ancient palaces reveal intricate mural work (below), while the carved dog (left) must have been an ancestor of the dalmation. Preceding pages: In a vintage map, Seoul is depicted as a walled fortress.*

ty formally pledges allegiance to the Ch'ing rulers.
**1704** — King Sukjong begins reconstruction, once again, of the city walls. The work takes eight years to complete.
**1846** — Kim Dae-gon, Korea's first Catholic priest, is martyred at Saenamt'o, a district in Seoul next to the Han River.
**1876** — Foreign ships begin using Inch'ŏn Harbor for trade and commerce.
**1882** — Korea enters the era of modern diplomacy when the Kingdom of Chosŏn establishes formal relations with the United States.
**1884** — A modern postal service begins operations.
**1897** — In an effort to establish its independence from a weakened China and to fend off pressure from Japan and the West, King Kojong declares Korea to be an empire with himself as emperor.
**1897** — The railroad between Seoul and the port of Inch'ŏn is built.
**1900** — A railroad bridge is built over the Han River, linking Seoul by rail to the southernmost parts of the Korean peninsula.
**1901** — Seoul's electricity supply is switched on.
**1903** — The Seoul YMCA is founded. The YMCA organization has played an important role in

Korea's modern social and political movements.
**1904** — The first modern hospital in Seoul, Che-jungwŏn — later renamed Severance Hospital — is founded by missionaries.
**1908** — Seoul gets its first running water system. Large sections of the old city wall are torn down to make room for the development of a contemporary capital, in the downtown area.
**1910** — Japan formally annexes Korea, opening a dark chapter in Korean history. The Japanese colonial government attempts to obliterate an independent Korean cultural identity, but fails.
**1912** — An electric trolley system begins operation on Ŭlchi-ro.
**1919** — Korea is rocked by student demonstrations that begin downtown in Pagoda Park touching off the now-celebrated March 1 Independence Movement. The Japanese ruthlessly crush the protests.
**1926** — The railroad bridge over the Han River is washed away in a great flood.
**1928** — The first public bus line begins operation in the streets of the city.
**1936** — Seoul's population reaches 600,000.
**1945** — The surrender of Japan on August 15 marks the end of 35 years of harsh colonial rule. A U.S.

MURAL DECORATIONS IN OLD PALACE

25

military government is established in Seoul for South Korea while Soviet troops occupy the North.

**1946** — Seoul becomes the official name of the capital. Seoul National University, destined to become the nation's most prestigious institute of higher education, is established.

**1948** — The fiery nationalist, Syngman Rhee, becomes Korea's first president. The first of five national constitutions that have been in effect since liberation is instituted.

**1950** — North Korea launches an attack on South Korea on June 25, and quickly occupies Seoul. The South retakes the city in heavy fighting on September 28, following the brilliant Inch'ŏn landing by General Douglas MacArthur. The city changes hands two more times during the war and is almost completely destroyed and depopulated.

**1953** — An armistice ends the fighting, but troop positions are frozen and the hostilities of the Korean War are never officially ended.

**1954** — Korea's first television broadcasts begin in a station operating in Seoul.

**1960** — The refusal of troops to fire on demonstrating students marching on the Blue House in Seoul forces the collapse of the government of President Syngman Rhee following a rigged election. The peaceful overthrow of the government raises hopes for democracy and launches students to the center of the political stage.

**1961** — Korean democracy collapses in a military coup led by Colonel Park Chung-hee, who rules Korea for the next 18 years.

**1968** — The last trolley lines in Seoul are torn up and removed. Construction of a modern highrise apartment and office development begins on Yŏ'ui-do, an island in the Han River. This initiates the massive expansion of the city south of the river.

**1972** — Promulgation of the Yushin Constitution, aimed at strengthening the authority of President Park, provokes widespread student protest. The city's population exceeds six million.

**1974** — The first subway line begins operating along Chong-no. Lines are gradually added on until a grid is completed a decade later.

**1975** — The National Assembly moves into a huge domed building on Yŏ'ui-do Island, beginning a gradual exodus of major institutions from the center of the city.

**1978** — The Sejong Cultural Center is opened, providing downtown Seoul with an impressive

and entertaining performing arts complex.

**1979** — President Park Chung-hee is assassinated on October 26 by the head of his own CIA. His death is the catalyst for a period of political instability. Eventually, General Chun Doo-hwan seizes control during fighting at the army headquarters in Seoul on December 12.

**1980** — Chun Doo-hwan extends his control over the national government. He becomes the President of Korea's Fifth Republic.

**1981** — The International Olympic Committee selects Seoul as the host of the 1988 Summer Olympics. The decision is seen as international recognition of Seoul's growing prominence and economic success and South Korea's acceptance in the family of nations.

**1982** — The night curfew in Seoul is lifted for the first time since the Korean War, ending the midnight scramble to get home. School uniforms are abolished. Professional baseball begins.

**1983** — A television marathon unexpectedly leads to reunification of hundreds of families separated during the Korean War more than 30 years earlier, ushering in an emotionally-wrenching year for Korea. Later, a Korean Airlines 747 passenger jet is shot down by the Soviet Union, killing all 269 persons on board. Finally, much of the Korean cabinet is killed in a North Korean bomb blast in Rangoon, forcing President Chun to return home nearly alone to form a new government.

**1984** — Government offices begin moving south of the city to Kwach'on. Pope John Paul II pays a visit to South Korea.

**1985** — The opening of the 63-story Daehan Life Insurance Building, Asia's tallest at the time, seems to symbolize the rise in importance of the city.

**1986** — The Olympic Park is finished. Successful staging of the Asian Games raises anticipation for the 1988 Olympics. The National Museum reopens in the newly-furbished Capitol Building which had served as the seat of the government for 50 years.

**1987** — The population of the city hurtles rapidly towards the 10-million mark while a new crop of Korean-made cars on the streets symbolizes Seoul's growing prosperity. Violent student demonstrations centered in Seoul force President Chun to reopen negotiations with the political opposition for a return to full democracy and free elections. In another gesture of conciliation, he declares an amnesty for hundreds of political prisoners.

Seoul has four distinct seasons and short spells of extreme hot and cold. In the summer after the seasonal *changma* rains, that turn the skies gray from mid-June to mid-July, the sun comes out and bakes the city, pushing temperatures into the high 30s on the Centigrade scale and sending Seoulites scrambling to the beaches.

In the winter, successive waves of cold weather roll out of Siberia with a ferocious

frozen punch that sends the mercury falling below −20 degrees Centigrade. Gusty dry winds further heighten the chill factor. During such spells, Koreans stay close to the floor. Following ancient tradition, even modern apartments are heated by an *ondol* floor heating system. Old habits die hard.

The only innovation is that hot water pipes have replaced the floor flues that carried hot smoke from the fire. Smoke flues are still used for heating in many old houses. That means a window must be open to prevent asphyxiation. To understand how wonderful sitting on a hot *ondol* floor can feel, just find yourself a breezy room

*Korean clothing provides some indication of social status. Country musicians often dress colorfully (above) and a television star (right), portraying a servant, wears a plain garment common among domestic workers in bygone days.*

on one of Seoul's winter days. But be forewarned. The floor may be hot enough to bake your bottom.

If the sultry summers and bitterly dry cold winters are misery in Korea, the lovely fall and spring seasons certainly make up for them. The warm and sunny days of spring are only occasionally marred by strong winds that blow in gusts of yellow dust all the way from China's Gobi Desert, a thousand miles away. Autumn is blessed with clear high skies that seem to expand the very scope of life itself.

When the first frosts turn the hillsides to scarlet and yellow, farmers begin driving into the city in trucks packed with produce. The markets then overflow with mounds of Chinese cabbage. The annual *kimch'i*-making ritual will provide each household with a supply of condiments and vitamins throughout the winter.

Like their country's climate, the people of Korea are prone to extremes. "The trouble with Koreans is that they don't like anything lukewarm — only scalding hot or freezing cold," says one local politician.

Although the remark was directed at the fact that Korean politicians have difficulty reaching amicable compromises, it can easily apply to most other aspects of life. From the frenetic devotion of newly-converted Christians whose mournful prayers can be heard throughout the night in the hills north of the city to the pungent taste of a cuisine laced with chilies, raw garlic, salt and vinegar, Koreans show little tendency towards moderation in anything.

When Koreans work, they seem to draw energy from some infinite reservoir. They pump every last ounce of strength into their task, regardless of any obstacles in their path. If they collapse in failure, they pick themselves up, and, undeterred, try again. Eventually, most succeed.

This spirit is no more apparent than in the growth of Seoul. Its resurrection from the near total destruction caused by the Korean War has been accomplished so fast that foreigners are sometimes bewildered by the apparently haphazard, unplanned accumulation of individually brilliant ideas that comprise the city. But Koreans love Seoul, its sheer immensity and the speed with which it has bestowed the benefits of modern living on so many of them. Most of all, Koreans love Seoul because it is the nerve center of their nation, the place where everything of importance occurs.

***Seoul's cultural life*** *offers a rich mixture of classical Korean and contemporary Western art forms. Above, a troupe of classically-trained musicians performs ancient Korean court music at the prestigious National Theater on Mt. Nam-san.*

31

O n the surface, Seoul's remarkable development may appear to have been bumpy. Indeed, a closer look reveals that its baptism into the contemporary world has been cruel and traumatic.

Precisely 200 years after the founding of the Yi Dynasty, Japanese invaders devastated the capital. Like Spartacus' gladiators in Rome, Korean slaves took advantage of the chaos and burned down the Kyŏngbok Palace in order to destroy the evidence of their menial status. The "liberation" proved short-lived for most, however. Unable to find an alternative to indentured servitude to support themselves, many of the slaves returned to their masters.

Eventually, the Japanese invaders were driven out and the capital rebuilt. But the arrival of the Western colonial powers prompted Japan to embark on a hasty course of modernization in the late 19th century. Once again Japan became a nemesis. Korea sought shelter under China's wing, a strategy that proved disastrous. When China lost a naval encounter with Japan in 1895, Korea lost its only means of protecting itself from Japanese manipulation. The Russo-Japanese War of 1905 sealed Korea's fate. Japan formally annexed the Korean peninsula in 1910, then attempted to obliterate all traces of Korean identity and independence.

In the process, the Japanese tried to erase the symbols of Korean authority. Of the more than 500 buildings in the Kyŏngbok Palace, the Japanese destroyed all but ten. Ch'anggyŏng Palace was demoted from a *kung,* palace, to a public *won,* park. A zoo and a greenhouse were installed and the grounds of the compound were planted extensively with cherry trees which blossom with the national flower of Japan.

In 1897, during the the reign of King Kojong, Korea had made a feeble attempt to declare itself an empire, independent of China. The king built a temple of heaven and altar patterned on the famous one in China; it eventually became a symbol of nationhood. The temple was dismantled by the Japanese in 1910. In its place, they built Korea's first luxury hotel, the Chosun Hotel. Today, a modern hotel with the same name occupies the site. The hotel's Ninth

*Traditional festivals in Seoul and other parts of the country swirl with color, sounds and symbols of the past. Such events occasionally get so intense, a mesmerized performer might inadvertently puncture his instrument (right) but continue right on playing.*

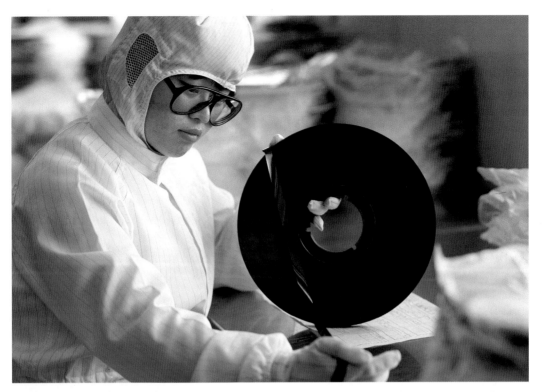

*As in neighboring Japan, advanced technology has played a major role in South Korea's rapid rise into the ranks of the world's industrial powers. Hi-tech components, many of them manufactured locally (above, top), are used in motor vehicle factories (above, bottom), television stations (left) and elsewhere.*

Gate Restaurant rests on the spot where the old temple had stood and has a splendid view of the altar, which remains intact.

In a space cleared in the Kyŏngbok Palace grounds, the Japanese built the huge Capitol Building. The neo-renaissance style structure came to symbolize Japanese colonial domination, partly because it destroyed the magical geomantic design of the old palace grounds as well as their beauty.

Korean troops managed to take the city twice. The first time they were pushed out by close combat in the streets of Seoul and in the surrounding mountains. When Chinese troops suddenly entered the war, Seoul was lost again to Communist occupation. When North Korea was pushed out a second time a few months later they burned the Namdae-mun, the Great South Gate, and the gate to the Kyŏngbok Palace — the

Koreans often debated whether to tear down the old Capitol when they regained independence after World War II. But the building was left standing. It now houses the National Museum.

There are other landmarks of the colonial era as well: Seoul City Hall, the Bank of Korea, and the Seoul Railroad Station. But nothing from Japan's colonial era inspires much affection among Koreans despite the historical role Japan played in bringing Seoul into the modern age. In any case, most of Seoul was destroyed during the tumultuous years of the Korean War.

During that conflict, Communist North

Kwanghwa-mun. Within 30 years, both gates not only had been entirely rebuilt and designated national treasures but engulfed by wide boulevards and tall office blocks.

The symbolic center of modern Seoul is City Hall Plaza. To call this a traffic circle would be an abuse of the English language. It is more like a traffic engineer's nightmare: seven feeder roads merge into a maze of turnabouts around a small fountain. It is the best and the worst of Seoul, a brilliant, if improvised, solution to the insoluble. Korean ingenuity always triumphs.

The four-story granite City Hall building with its prominent stepped dome and digital clock, still dominates the plaza in spite of the profusion of skyscrapers. It would be stretching the point to describe the structure as beautiful. Completed by the Japanese in 1926, it is modeled on the Imperial Diet

*The development of Seoul into an economic capital has fueled the construction of office towers, highrise apartments, and other projects. Above, workers check blueprints for the Olympic Stadium, the center of world sporting power in 1988.*

Building in Tokyo and still has about it a faint air of colonial diffidence and bureaucratic arrogance.

Across the way, one of Seoul's earliest first-class establishments, the towering Plaza Hotel, faces City Hall. Each year more buildings are torn down to make room for such modern steel and glass spires. Behind the Plaza are the remnants of a Chinatown that once hummed with life.

lic heart of the nation. The feeder road that leads to this gate is at least 15 lanes wide and teems with traffic from early morning until late at night. It is called Sejong-no after the Yi Dynasty king who contributed so much to Korean culture.

Looking out over the Kwanghwa-mun intersection several hundred yards south of the gate, atop a tall granite pedestal, is a bronze statue of Korea's greatest military

South Korea has a sizeable Chinese minority. Many people sought refuge here from the impoverished Shantung province across the Yellow Sea. However, the Chinese in Korea have never emerged as a dominant merchant class as they have in the rest of Asia. On the contrary, they comprise a kind of underclass of restaurateurs and storekeepers who are often barred from the mainstream of Korean life. In what's left of Chinatown, you will find a few of their drab restaurants serving the most authentic, unKoreanized Chinese dumplings, *man-du,* in town. Spiraling property prices coupled with the demand for downtown office space may put an end to these establishments as well, however.

If City Hall Plaza is the symbolic heart of the city, then it is the Kwanghwa-mun beneath Pugak Mountain that is the symbo-

strategist, Admiral Yi Sun-sin (1545–98). Admiral Yi has the distinction of being the man Koreans admire most, according to local Gallup polls, an uncontroversial symbol of nationalism who was resurrected and reshaped into a modern-style hero by the late President Park Chung-hee. The admiral invented the world's first armor-clad vessel, the *kŏbuk-sŏn* or "turtle ship," which he used to achieve stunning victories over the much-larger Japanese navy when it invaded Korean waters in 1592 and 1597.

City Hall Plaza and the Kwanghwa-mun intersection may seem larger than life but once you get off the main avenues, Seoul

*College students* *brandish guitars and grins as they make their way to a singing session at one of Seoul's many small cafes and coffee houses* *(above). Collegiate musical tastes range from American hits to homespun protest ballads.*

# Antiques to Order

**B**yun Kyong-sook waved good-bye to a Korean matron outside her cluttered basement shop in Insa-dong. "She really got away with a bargain," she said, wiping her brow.

The "bargain" was a beautiful replica of an antique *ham*, a wedding box, copied from a piece in a prestigious private collection in Seoul. The box will be sent to the house of a bride in exchange for a sizeable dowry.

Mrs Byun, a patient 52-year-old mother of two adolescent boys, has made a modest business from her efforts to preserve a centuries-old tradition of fine furniture-making that has been threatened by the flood of mass machine-produced goods. When the supply of exquisite antique furniture from the Korean countryside began drying up in the late 70s, many dealers went out of business. Others hung on by raising their prices or selling low-quality pieces that were sometimes assembled from old wood.

Mrs Byun took a more original approach to keep her business afloat. She took a master carpenter into the storerooms of the National Folklore Museum where together they studied the construction of the finest pieces of antique Korean furniture. Then she began making exact replicas in a small studio outside Seoul. Her goal was not to add more fakes to the country's crowded copycat market but to produce a line of classically-styled Korean furniture at affordable prices.

"When I started my antique business in the 60s, Insa-dong, or Mary's Alley as it was known to Westerners, was the center of Seoul's antique business. Korean chests were very cheap then," Mrs Byun says.

"We Koreans were broke in the decade after the War," she continues. "We were only too glad to exchange our antiques and heirlooms for money. We traded our old chests to buy daily necessities and to send our sons to college. Before the War, our antiques went to Japan, after the War they went to Europe and America."

When the Korean economy gained momentum in the late 60s and 70s, Korean intellectuals, artists and members of the beau monde finally had the money to begin buying back the culture that was sold for a song a decade earlier.

"That was the golden period in my business," Mrs Byun recalls. "My customers were enlightened people with whom I shared knowledge about the folk objects and wood antiques in my shop. As soon as I

**Byun Kyong-sook (left)** is one of the entrepreneurs in Seoul who has tried to halt the decline in the production of Korea's exquisite classical furniture. She specializes in making and selling exact replicas of antiques **(below).**

*sold something to one client, I would buy something else and invite another patron to come enjoy it with me. Because I preferred selling to people I liked, I never made much money. But I had a lot of fun."*

*The pleasantries soon ended, however. By the middle of the 1970s, a new monied class fueled by land speculation began buying antiques solely for their value as an investment.*

*"I was demoralized by those nouveau riche speculators who bought antiques without knowing them," Mrs Byun complains. "They would visit my shop, ask for my most expensive pieces and buy them right up. The next time the pieces came to market, they were priced beyond my reach."*

*In the late 70s, the triple murder of prominent Insa-dong dealer, Chong Hae-sok, and his wife and chauffeur, put a chill on the Korean antique market. The murders were never solved but a lengthy police investigation of all Insa-dong dealers and their clients scared away the respectable collectors who used antiques as a discreet means of hiding their wealth. In addition, a recession caused by the steep rise in oil prices had dried up some of the ready reserves of cash. Finally, the flow of fine antiques from the countryside had dwindled to a trickle by then.*

*Unwilling to forsake her love of Korean woodcrafts, Mrs Byun decided to begin manufacturing replicas after receiving encouragement from former public figures like National Museum of Korea Director, Choi Sunu, and Space Theater architect, Kim Swoo-geun. Eventually, some of her masterly reproductions of rare pieces found their way to Korea's overseas cultural missions which couldn't have otherwise afforded the price of a genuine antique.*

*Mrs Byun has not given up the antique business entirely, however. Her knowledge of Seoul's private collections still attracts people who need advice on buying or selling old furniture. The prices of exquisite pieces, particularly those used in the studios and sitting rooms of the old class of scholars, now trade for thousands of dollars. On the other hand, some wooden artifacts that came out of the women's quarters or from the kitchens of old middle-class homes can still be picked up at bargain prices of a few hundred dollars.*

*For those wishing to take home a piece of the Korean heritage as a souvenir of their visit, other good buys recommended by Mrs Byun include old blanket chests, rice and bean chests, food trays, cookie presses, and mirror boxes.*

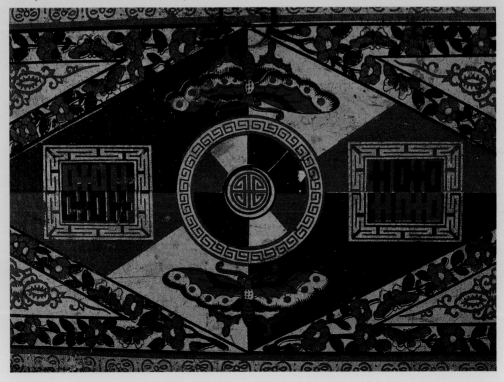

puts on a human face. Moving east from the Kwanghwa-mun intersection down Chong-no, the sidewalks bustle with crowds of shoppers parading in front of smart-looking storefronts that display goods ranging from camping gear to books and electronic products. Nearly all of it is made in Korea.

One long block east of the intersection is Pohin-gak, the bell platform that once marked the physical center of the city. The

bell was rung at dawn and again at dusk to signal the opening and closing of the city gates. Nowadays a new bell, the replacement for the original which cracked in 1984, is used only to ring in the new year.

This was the bell that gave Chong-no its name as "Chong" means "bell" in Korean. Chong-no is still the city's main east–west thoroughfare. It leads straight from the government district to what was once the largest market in all of Asia — the Dongdae-mun Sijang, or Great East Gate Market. Strictly speaking, Dongdae-mun covers just one city block, but it is the anchor of dozens of wholesale specialized markets.

***Gushy period dramas** about romance and courtly intrigue are a mainstay of Korean television. An actor, dressed in the princely robes of the Yi Dynasty, waits for his cue (**left**). Another demonstrates traditional Korean dance (**above**).*

# The Buddha's Birthday

**E**ach spring all of Seoul enjoys a special treat. At that time the people celebrate the "Coming of the Buddha," a national holiday that falls on the eighth day of the fourth lunar month, usually in early May.

The associated festivities are a kind of cross between New Orleans' Mardi Gras and Hinduism's "Festival of Lights." That makes Buddha Shakyamuni's birthday celebration one of the most visible and colorful of Korea's traditional holidays.

The highlight of the celebration is the lantern procession. As dusk falls, crowds of people from old grandmothers and college students to pre-school children don their national dress — the gaily-colored hanbok. Then they parade through the streets of Seoul carrying lighted lanterns to their favorite temples. At the temples, they attach their names to the lanterns, make a wish, and hang them in a spot they consider to be lucky.

To the Buddhist, the lantern symbolizes wisdom and mercy. Its light is believed to have the power to brighten and eradicate the dark spots of life.

In bygone days, lanterns were made of silk or paper. But plastic or nylon versions can now be purchased for the occasion, then used in the home afterwards. They come in a variety of auspicious plant and animal shapes: the lotus, carp, drum, turtle and pear are among the most popular. There is even a garlic-shaped lantern, in the improbable event that you forget that passion of the national appetite.

Only about one-third of South Korea's populace still subscribes to the Buddhist faith. But come the

"Coming," everybody is a Buddhist. The whole of Seoul seems to come out into the warm spring night for a breath of the carnival atmosphere.

In the suburbs, families or group of friends pack food and charcoal burners and, of course, plenty of soju wine. They picnic along the paths and riverbanks that lead to the big temples. Groups of middle-aged women dance, sing and drink the night away under the moonlight. This is the one of the rare days when they can take a break from the neverending demands of the home and family.

Preparations for the Buddha's birthday begin weeks in advance. At each temple in the country, teams of volunteers take over one of the main halls, where they make the lanterns that are to be sold and carried in the procession. The choicest lanterns are festooned on every building and tree in the temple grounds or strung along the path leading to the temple. Neighborhoods with Buddhist temples, however modest, are decked out days ahead of the event.

On the day itself, hordes of devotees and onlookers crowd into the temple precincts to pray and take in the sights. The monks unfurl 15-meter high religious paintings, the only day each year when public viewing is permitted. They perform characteristically Buddhist dances to Buddhist music. Sometimes groups of devotees perform a taptori, a ritual in which believers led by a monk form a ring and circle a tap, or pagoda, chanting sutras and offering prayers.

The big crowds begin arriving at 7 p.m. By 10, each temple complex is ablaze with the light of thousands of lanterns, a sea of flickering and bobbing multi-colored stars that seems to have drifted down from the heavens.

In Seoul, the grandest parade of lanterns begins at Yŏ'ui-do Plaza after sunset and ends downtown at the Chogye-sa, the head temple of South Korea's largest Buddhist sect, around midnight. This procession includes colorful floats built and manned by activist students from Buddhist universities.

The merrymaking breaks up around 3 o'clock in the morning as weary monks climb ladders to take down the lanterns, now barely flickering. Some of the lantern frames are saved for use in the next year's celebrations. By daybreak the timeless quiet of their temple abode returns. The spring of 1988, the year of the Olympics, marks the 2,532th birthday of the Buddha.

The best temples at which to enjoy the birthday celebrations are the scenic Tosŏn-sa in U'i-dong in the northern suburbs of Seoul and Pongŭn-sa near the KOEX building, south of the Han River. The most lively celebrations occur at Chogye-sa downtown, Pŏngwŏn-sa near Yonsei University and Pomun-sa near Korea University.

**Each spring,** thousands of painted, lighted lanterns **(below)** blossom throughout South Korea as the country celebrates the birthday of the Buddha. Devotees hang their lanterns in their favorite temples, then pray for good fortune **(left).**

Dongdae-mun Sijang can take days to explore and visitors who invest the time and effort are in for some surprises. On one street, you'll find nothing but stores selling tape: one sells masking tape, another packing tape, yet another electrical tape. There are industrial cookware, electronics and computer tape markets at the Seun Arcade.

The East Gate also has the best bargains on Korean bedding, fabrics of every description and composition, and the cheapest imaginable ready-made clothing, some selling for a fraction of the price asked for in fashionable stores downtown. Prices are extremely low because many of Seoul's small garment factories operate in the East Gate area, often located right above the wholesale outlets.

The Seoul of the East Gate area is a throwback to another era, an anachronism. It has no modern, wide avenues ostentatiously designed to prove that South Korea has made incredible progress since the war. This great wholesale bazaar seems more like a rural fair gone wild. The thousands and thousands of tiny shops that line the labyrinth of narrow corridors are stuffed so full of merchandise that they appear poised to assault everyone that passes by. And if the goods themselves miss the mark, the shopkeepers are quick on the uptake. Few people in the world are more natural or more friendly salesmen.

Truck access to the downtown markets has become increasingly difficult and traffic jams are interminable. Gradually, the city government is trying to move the wholesale markets to the city's outskirts to relieve congestion. But the slow process never seems to have much impact. In the meantime, the markets remain a delightful way to discover how most Koreans still do business and where most go for a bargain.

The upmarket crowd, on the other hand, congregates in fashionable Myŏng-dong. Here, well-known Korean fashion designers like Kim Chang-suk, Lee Shin-u, and Han Hye-ja display local renditions of haute couture in swanky shops. And in the basements and around the corner in the alleyways are the bars and coffee shops where many of the city's business transactions take place.

*Fine Chinese calligraphy was prized by Korea's old Confucian elite, but the art is sadly neglected by a younger, Westernized generation. At right, an elderly man in exquisite Korean silk practices the art on the* ondol *floor of an old house.*

Across the avenue from Myǒng-dong are Seoul's three most prestigious downtown department stores — the Lotte, Midopa and Shinsegae. On days leading up to holidays the area is literally impassable. Thousands of shoppers block access as they stock up on supplies from gift sets of instant coffee to expensive cuts of choice beef, something of which the Korean palate never tires.

Koreans are easily seduced by a famous label or fine shopping bag. The Christian Diors, Yves St. Laurents and their ilk may one day control the market for fine goods in Seoul, as they already do in Tokyo. But first they must overcome import barriers which still enable the market to be dominated by home-grown brands such as Bando Fashions or Kolon Mode for men and Morado or Lee's originals for women. Happily, the quality of Korean-designed and manufac-

tured goods is rapidly improving.

Myǒng-dong is also Seoul's financial district, the hub of its moneylenders, finance companies, stockbrokers, banks, and even black market moneychangers. This reservoir of capital has helped fuel an economic machine that has achieved a remarkable average growth rate of 8.5 per cent annually during the past 25 years. But Myǒng-dong also hosted the great loan scandals that repeatedly rocked Seoul in the early 1980s. Now, however, many security houses have moved to Yǒ'ui-do, the island in the Han River, to be close to the Stock Exchange and to escape downtown's high rents.

*Old pines enhance the grounds of the Kyǒngbok Palace; the multi-tiered pagoda once housed the National Museum (left). Confucian ritual, including ancestor worship (above), remains important despite inroads made by Christianity.*

***The Kunjong-jon,*** *the Throne Hall of Kyŏngbok Palace* (**above**)*, was the center of power throughout Korea. The palace was completed in 1395 when the Yi Dynasty was at the height of its glory. Today, it stands neglected and deteriorating like a mausoleum to an age that's fast receding from memory.*

Nestling conspicuously among the glittering shops and finance houses is the Myŏng-dong Cathedral, headquarters of South Korea's Catholic Archdiocese. Christianity has swept through Korea like a brush fire in front of a hot wind fanning the growing social and political importance of the Church. While most of the recent converts have been Protestants, the Archdiocese still leads the largest group of organized Christians. Thus, when Stephen Cardinal Kim Sou Hwan speaks on any subject — whether it is the abuse of prisoners in Korean jails or the need for constitutional reform — he commands a moral authority unmatched by any other Korean. For this reason, the Cathedral is the site of pilgrimages from nearly all of the nation's top politicians, whether they represent the left, the right or those that cautiously stick to the middle-of-the-road.

Christianity's rise has been spectacular in South Korea. Nearly one-third of a nation that once subscribed to Buddhism has already been converted to the newer faith.

*Although the number of supermarkets in Seoul is on the rise, most Koreans still shop at colorful open-air markets. At one corner of Chegi-dong Market merchants sell garlic (left) while nearby a bean seller guards his neat displays (above).*

# Pickled Heat

Just before the first snows of autumn each year, Korea's farmers harvest the cabbage and radish from their fields and deliver them by the truckloads to Seoul. Suddenly, the pavements of the city's sprawling open-air markets fill up with mountains of produce. As if on cue, housewives descend in droves on the markets to inspect the bounty. They haggle ruthlessly for the best price, then haul home a supply of vegetables for the winter. So begins the annual ritual of kimjang — the making of kimch'i.

Kimch'i is Korea's national food. The label covers any pickled vegetable but is generally used to refer to Chinese cabbage and long white radish which has been fermented in a savory brine of salt, chili, peppers and garlic. Seasonings such as ginger, scallions and seafood including baby shrimps, oysters and anchovies are often also added to the basic recipe, depending on the chef's taste and the size of the family bank account.

Needless to say, kimch'i is an acquired taste. Some foreigners never develop a liking for the fiery mixture. But those who do often become even bigger addicts than the Koreans, who claim that they just can't digest their meals without a side dish or two.

In fact, science confirms that claim. During the fermentation process, lactic acid forms in the mixture; its ingestion helps to sterilize the digestive tract. Kimch'i also aids in digestion itself in much the same way as soured milk or yoghurt used in other countries. A serving of kimch'i each day doesn't do much for one's breath, but it does supply the body's daily minimum requirement of Vitamin C.

The preparation of kimch'i has a practical side; it has traditionally served as a preservation method that enables a household to have enough vegetables until the first fresh greens reach the market the next spring. But making kimch'i is a massive task. For a family of five, the homemaker has to buy some 100 heads each of cabbage and long radish, five kilograms of chili peppers, three kilograms of garlic, 20 liters of salt and proportionately large amounts of any other seasonings or spices needed for her own secret recipe. The expense of such a large order is a major drawback, however. Preparing enough kimch'i for the season puts such a strain on a family's budget that no husband dares come home during the fall unless he has a kimjang bonus from his boss.

Once the ingredients have been purchased, a

**Red hot** chili peppers, sold from bushels at Seoul's open-air markets **(left),** are a prime ingredient of the national dish, *kimchi.* During the winter, earthern-ware jars of *kimchi* are stored in the ground **(below).**

*homemaker summons all the free female hands in the house. Thus begins the laborious process of washing, slicing and salting the mounds of cabbage and radish to be fermented. The women mince the red chilies, blend them with the other spices and sea-sonings, and pour this potent mixture onto the pre-pared vegetables. The lot is then carefully placed into large earthenware pots that are sealed and buried up to their necks in the yard. If the family lives in a flat, the pots are stacked on the balcony, next to drying laundry. The combination of winter cold and hot spices keeps* kimch'i *crunchy and prevents it from spoiling.*

*Although* kimch'i *can be eaten as soon as it is made, like red wine it tastes a bit young. As it matures and is consumed through the winter months, it acquires character; its bouquet and aftertaste may even attract compliments.*

*In South Korea's male-dominated society, a woman's worth is still measured in some quarters by her skill at producing sons — and at making delicious* kimch'i*; and the reputation of a family's kitchen is often judged on the quality of the* kimch'i *served to guests. No matter how pretty or well-educated a woman is, a bride isn't considered to have been properly raised unless she can put a tasty plate of homemade* kimch'i *on her husband's table.*

*Along with boiled rice and soup,* kimch'i *is the mainstay of a typical meal, but it hasn't always been part of the Korean diet. Although its principal ingredients, cabbage and white radish, were culti-vated by the Chinese as early as 1,000 BC, Koreans only started to "kimch'i" these two vegetables in the 17th century. It was then that the main seasoning for the dish, the red chili pepper, was introduced to the Korean peninsula.*

*With the increasing supply of hot-house vegetables throughout the winter months and the cramped storage space on apartment balconies, the people of Seoul eat less* kimch'i *than they did a decade ago. But modern culinary influences will never completely eliminate their fondness for their spicy hot pickled speciality. A meal simply isn't a meal without it.* Kimch'i *is such a part of the taste and culture, they have even opened a* Kimch'i *Museum (28-27 Pil-dong, near Korea House in downtown Seoul; tele-phone, 277-0791), where visitors can sample many delicious varieties of this delicacy.*

The Christian religion has helped many cope with the confusing social changes caused by rapid industrialization and the massive migration from villages to the city. The movement has been led for the most part by politically-conservative, Bible-thumping preachers, who bear an uncanny resemblance to American evangelists. They tell their congregations that the rewards of faith can be found in this lifetime, not just the

viewed with disfavor for many years, Shamanism recently has enjoyed an officially-sanctioned revival of sorts; the government now plays it up as a kind of art form.

Shamans are mediums who call back the souls of the dead to help solve the problems of the living. They dance, they wail, they speak in tongues. Hours, often days, later, when it is all over, the living are reputed to have been freed from the burden of a dead

next. They tell the faithful to work hard, make money and succeed. That may not always come naturally to a people steeped in self-effacing Confucian, Buddhist and Shamanist traditions.

For an eye-opening look at the new Christianity, attend the stunning show at the Full Gospel Church each Sunday morning. With a congregation it claims to total more than 500,000, reputedly the largest in the world, each service takes the entertaining form of a multi-media show simultaneously translated into a variety of languages in various parts of the church.

Devout Christians can also be heard wailing to the Lord in mournful prayer in the hills of Samgak-san above P'yŏngch'ang-dong, north of the city, night and day. The practice is an offshoot of Shamanist ritual that is still widespread. Indeed, after being

soul who has brought unhappiness.

Despite Christianity's inroads and Shamanism's lingering influences, Buddhism is South Korea's largest organized religion. It has inspired some of the country's greatest art and architecture. Much of it can be seen in the old temples that still survive outside of Seoul or in the figures carved out of granite on the hillsides of the city.

Buddhism is also the source of Seoul's most colorful festival. On the Buddha's birthday every spring, a mile-long procession of people carrying painted lanterns marches from the island of Yŏ'ui-do to Chongye-sa, a large temple in downtown Seoul.

*On Buddha's Birthday temples unfurl religious paintings like this one at Pŏngwon-sa (left). A young father in blue-jeans bundles up his son against the bitter winter cold as an old man in a traditional fur overcoat strolls by (above.)*

One of the last refuges of tranquil, traditional Korean atmosphere amid the crowded clamor of the capital can be found at the Undang Yŏgwan. Here, a young couple share a rare moment of privacy **(below)** in the inn's cozy courtyard.

# Loving the Yŏgwan

The days of Korea's traditional inn, the yŏgwan, are numbered in Seoul. Spectacular surges in downtown land prices and hefty increases in taxes have made them unprofitable and driven most out of business. In fact, the last of downtown Seoul's yŏgwan, the Undang, is losing money but its owners have balked at closing down.

"For us, it's a matter of pride," says Yi Chong-dae, manager of Seoul's venerable Undang Yŏgwan.

Set around several cozy courtyards, the Undang has 31 rooms in single-story, tile-roofed units. The owner of the 30-odd-year-old inn is Miss Pak Kwi-hui, who is considered a veritable living National Treasure because of her mastery of the kayagum, Korea's 12-string zither.

Despite economic problems, Yi said Miss Pak is unwilling to change things at Undang Yŏgwan. In fact, the inn has a loyal staff of 15 and she feels obligated to support them and their families for life. She believes the impersonal cement cubicles that now pass for inns all over the city just cannot compare with the traditional Korean inn.

Although the Undang does not make any pretensions of providing convenient modern services, it has bowed to some contemporary pressures: a communal shower with hot running water has been installed. The ordinary rooms are small but neat with paper-covered ondol floors that radiate heat throughout the chilly nights. A sheet metal wardrobe and a low table with a telephone on a doily are the only furniture; floral wallpaper, a calendar and a small wall mirror, the only decorations. Bedding consists of a padded

yol mattress, a quilted ibol blanket and a pyogae pillow stuffed with rice husks.

Needless to say, the Undang Yŏgwan, like all traditional Korean inns, is not tailored for the enjoyment of those who savor the privacy of a tiny room. Outside the room entrances is a traditional maru, a wooden verandah where guests sit and talk, or even chat with the friendly groundskeeper.

The only long-term resident, Miss Kong Ok-jim, occupies a large room reserved for honored guests. It faces south towards the enormous wooden gate of the compound. A distinguished folk dancer who specializes in mime, Miss Kong receives visits from her admiring fans and students till late in the night.

Room rates start at only W10,000 per night, so the inn is almost always full. It attracts an odd mix of guests including Korean construction workers from the provinces, Japanese students on tour, English teachers from Japan, and a motley crew of impoverished Korean poets and artists. The Undang's big social event of the year is the Korean finals of the world paduk, or go, championship. The winners go on to compete in the world championship in Japan.

In another refusal to bow to modern pressures, the Undang declines to rent rooms by the hour during the day. That cuts off potential revenue from the lucrative trade in hotel rooms for romantic afternoon trysts. "We run a clean place here," says Yi.

The cacophony begins each morning at six at the Undang at a long outdoor sink; it has several spigots for cold water and guests come to brush their teeth and splash the sleep out of their eyes here. A vat of hot water sits atop a heater beside the sink.

Miss Kong rises early. Dressed in a flowing white hanbok, she applies a toothbrush to her diamond ring as it reflects the crisp sunlight. Afterwards, a full-course Korean breakfast of rice, seasoned vegetables, kimch'i and a hearty toen-jang soybean soup is delivered to each room.

Dinner is served about 7:30 p.m., another delicious full-course Korean meal with soup, pulgogi, rice, kimch'i, and a plethora of side dishes. Between the clatter of kitchen staff washing dishes, the chatter of the train of guests who chug through the yŏgwan until late in the evening and the raucous music and laughter from the nearby nightclubs, the Undang may not be the place for anyone wishing to turn in early.

Mercifully, the clamor tapers off around midnight when the only sounds that can be heard are the patter of mice in the ceiling and the melodious calls of vendors hawking snacks in a distant alley. On the papered screen doors, the bright moonlight etches the outlines of some flowering bushes. Sleep comes to the Undang at last.

The Undang Yŏgwan is located at 79-1 Unni-dong, Chongno-ku; tel. 765-4194.

*Hiking up* the mountains on Seoul's outskirts is the national exercise; it's also one of the only ways of getting away from the pressures of the city for a jug of *soju,* a bowl of *kimchi* — and *thou* (**below**).

## Scaling the Heights

**B**lessed with rugged mountains inside and just outside the city limits that are fortunately too steep to be developed for commercial residential purposes, Seoul has become a haven for avid hikers and climbers. Thousands of Seoulites, with a characteristic burst of energy and determination, assault the hills each weekend. It's time to get out of the house and the city pollution, to get some exercise and blow off steam. The more style-conscious step into their knickerbockers, maybe pull on their red gaiters with white snowflakes and put on green hats with long plumes, take the pick off the wall and scramble up the mountains of Seoul at the first hint of a warm sunny day. So why not join the climb.

No hike is complete, however, without a 40-lb pack stuffed with all the fixings for an elaborate barbecue including grills, charcoal, marinated meat and kimch'i, not to forget ample quantities of beer or soju, South Korea's popular rice wine.

The mountains also come alive with the sound of music — solo and group performances. Don't be surprised if you hear a bit of yodeling. As the day wears on, and the soju bottles empty out, you may hear the full throttle of vocal chords echoing off a distant peak.

All this is not just a spontaneous outburst on the part of individuals. In fact, it's not unusual to run into a party of hikers numbering more than a hundred hiking through the old mountain fortress in Pukhan Mountain, the Pukhansan-sŏng. It may be a school outing or an excursion. Or it could be something else; one of Korea's most famous groups of trekkers is The Democratic Hiking Club, set up by prominent government opposition leader Kim Young-sam and his associates back in the years when they were banned from all political activity.

If some of the hikers appear to be trotting up the hills, they may be doing just that. Mountain-climbing derbies are regularly held in which participants race to place stamps on a scorecard as they reach each point on a mapped-out route.

The exhilirating hills of Seoul are easily accessible. Take a taxi to the Olympia Hotel in P'yŏngch'ang-dong, north of the city, then just follow the crowd up the slope across the road until you reach a trail head. This path leads to nearby temples or peaks.

If you are in good shape, you can take the long trail up to the Pukhan Fortress, then exit at U'i-dong to the east or through the West Gate near Kup'abal where there is easy access to the main roads. A shorter hike up from the Kugi Tunnel leads to Sŭngga-sa, a temple with a beautiful late 10th century Buddhist bas relief rock carving.

Other popular hiking spots include Tobong-san to the north and Namhansansŏng, the South Mountain Fortress, which is south of the Han River.

On the Buddha's birthday, temples through-out Seoul and the rest of the country, decked out in gorgeous colors, are visited by Koreans dressed in the sartorial splendor of their traditional *hanbok* clothing.

Although the festivities surrounding the Buddha's birthday are likely to persevere, Buddhism has been on the decline. The nearly unanimous devotion it once commanded has eroded, partly as a result of recent

established the proper Confucian hierarchy that governs how two people should interact with one another.

Such rigid etiquette often strikes for-eigners as absurd. Nevertheless, office workers usually cannot go home until the boss leaves — which is normally late in the evening. Thus, most Koreans can still be found at their desks after 7:30 p.m.

When the boss does leave, the whole

scandals including a murder among its monks and an ugly public struggle for the leadership of the largest sect, the Chogye.

Buddhism and all of the other professed faiths and spiritual beliefs have always seemed profoundly overshadowed by Con-fucianism, the Chinese ethical code that has deeply influenced society for the past 500 years. Urban living has taken its toll on the outward trappings of Confucianism such as the elaborate rituals of ancestor worship that are an important part of village society. Yet a foreigner's first brush with Confucian ethics can occur during something as simple as a routine introduction and exchange of business cards, always done with the right hand. The Korean will take the card and carefully scrutinize it for any titles that may be attached to the name. As a rule, Koreans are uncomfortable until they have clearly

office may follow him to a bar. Should an employee vent his frustrations by slugging his superior in the mouth during a drunken rage, all will be forgiven and forgotten the next morning. No matter how raucous the night, how bad the hangovers, or how bruis-ing the brawl everyone turns up bright, early and enthusiastic for work.

Another idiosyncrasy is the utterly blind deference to the elderly, even if the elder is just a few months older. It seems like an anachronism that ought to have been left behind in the villages of another era.

Yet Confucianism has provided a social glue that Koreans have used with incredible

*People joke* that clothes boutiques outnumber book-shops outside the Ewha Woman's University gates. That fashion consciousness flourishes at a showing of the latest evening wear from Japan as models prance down a catwalk at the Hyatt Hotel (**above and left**).

success to build large organizations. South Korea's huge industries have armies of factory and office workers. Like most other races on earth, Koreans have their own way of doing things and while it often seems peculiar, if not outright foolhardy, no one can scoff at their achievements.

As Seoul expanded to the south, life for the middle class became synonymous with occupying an apartment in one of the dozens of highrise complexes south of the Han River with a modest sedan in the car park and a supermarket just around the corner. Some of the city's newer and better public schools are located in this area as well. Ambitious parents slave, save and scheme as soon as a child is born so that they can move into one of Kang-nam's "good" neighborhoods where their youngster will have a chance to go to a prestigious school.

While these neighborhoods are not exactly charming in mood or appearance, they are neat and clean and prettified, more or less. The areas around Pangbae-dong near the Express Bus Terminal and Apkujŏng-dong are lit up with posh night life. At Kisaeng-style houses, exclusively for men, professional hostesses pop food and spoon drinks into the mouths of their pampered customers. Bars, clubs and cafes serve cocktails to the roar of all kinds of music from loud stereo systems and cater to swinging singles and dating couples.

Among the most popular establishments in Seoul, as they are in Tokyo, are the

*Traffic congestion on the city's streets continues to mount (left) as the car becomes more affordable for the average family. Although the city's workforce remains predominantly male, even women traffic force wardens are needed (above).*

61

*karaoke* "sing-along" bars where customers take turns passing around a microphone and belting out their favorite songs. There is also a collection of saunas and barber shops, standard fixtures in the cities of Asia. The government periodically launches a perpetually-fruitless crackdown on the provision of what it calls "lewd services," claiming it wants to put an end to wasteful consumption. Indeed, visitors should enter the saunas, barber shops and hostess clubs at their own risk, preferably with someone who knows the ropes — and has deep pockets lined with gold.

For the more adventurous or poverty-stricken male, Seoul has several cheap red light areas in the northeast districts. But they are far off the beaten track for foreigners — and better left there.

Less exotic forms of entertainment can be

found in It'ae-wŏn, the shopping, entertainment and residential district outside the main U.S. army post at Yongsan. The string of clubs feature distinctly American fare, from hard rock to country-and-western music. Many have even outgrown both the tastes and the pocketbooks of the American GIs who were the catalyst in the growth of the district, and increasing numbers of well-heeled Koreans are venturing into it.

All of It'ae-wŏn has thus turned upside-down in recent years. Once a conglomeration of stalls selling cheap merchandise of rather dubious origin and quality, it's now lush with dazzling modern shopping plazas.

---

*A **company's** executives select the winning entries in a children's art competition **(right)**. Meanwhile, entrepreneurs have been busy churning out caps **(above)** and other souvenirs in hopes of turning a profit from another competition, the Olympics.*

*A **South Korean** soccer coach lectures his team on the fine points of the game as preparations for the 1988 Olympics reached fever pitch years ahead of the event (**above**). The South Koreans hope to field strong teams in several events in order to win some gold medals before the home crowd in Seoul.*

By far, the greatest influence on Seoul's transformation in recent years has been the 1988 Olympic Games. Every Seoulite is intensely aware of the enormous symbolic importance of the event. New highways and bridges, not to mention the stadiums and playing fields where the Games will be held, have been named after the Olympics. A simple *p'al-p'al*, which translates simply as "88," is all one needs to say to evoke the spirit. Clock towers and government buildings throughout the city began counting down the days to the opening ceremonies years in advance with giant digital display boards and banners.

For a few weeks in 1988, the world will come to Seoul. It will be a giant coming-out party, of sorts, and Korean hospitality forbids that the least blade of grass should be out of place.

In 1988, Seoul hopes the world will finally recognize the achievements of a people who have built a modern metropolis from the ruins of an ancient city in just a single generation. It will be the time to pause for a few weeks, to share those accomplishments with thousands of visitors from abroad. Yet the physical manifestation of the capital city is not all that's likely to inspire the Olympics' guests and the others who follow in their wake. Even more impressive is the incredible energy, determination and creativity of a people who will finally take their rightful place among the great cultured nations of the world.

*The national rowing team grunts and grips the oars of a skiff during a pre-Olympics workout on the Han River (above). Even potential future Olympic hopefuls brush up on their tae kwon do (right).*

*The massive Asian Games,* the premier sporting event in the Far East, were hosted by Seoul in 1986. The colorful ceremonies staged by South Koreans from all walks of life as well as athletes competing in the Games provided a taste of the spectacular dance, music, costumes and color that's in store for the entire world when Seoul hosts the Olympics in 1988.

# Back of the Book

This section provides detailed information, exciting insights and entertaining tidbits about Seoul and is especially designed to enhance your travel experience. The main map depicts Greater Seoul; some of its principal sights, districts and physical characteristics. Little-known facts about the city from items on its ghostbusters to the ingredients for a nose omelette are revealed in Seoul Sidelights. The suggested sightseeing itineraries in Seoul Tours are accompanied by numbered maps that will help you get around to some of the most interesting attractions in and around the city on your own. Off the Beaten Track will enable you to travel where few tourists have ever traveled before, including No Man's Land. Best Bets is a digest of the best of everything Seoul has to offer. Finally, the Travel Notes summarize the essential basic information needed to get you to Seoul and back.

*The landmark Nam-san, or Seoul Tower, is a popular observation point for panoramic views of South Korea's bustling, burgeoning capital city. It looks like a beacon of the 21st Century towering over the modern office towers and apartment blocks.*

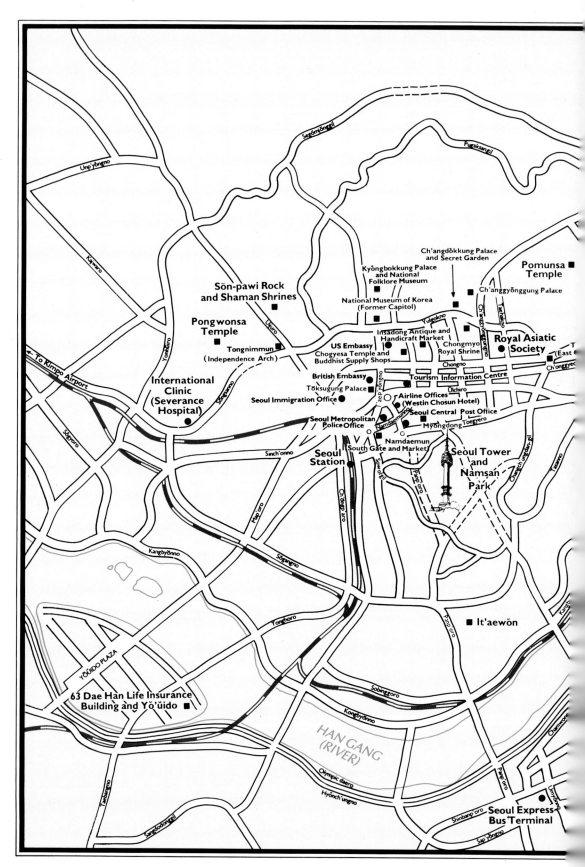

Sŏn-pawi Rock
and Shaman Shrines

Pongwonsa
Temple

Tongnimmun
(Independence Arch)

International
Clinic
(Severance
Hospital)

Serōmjŏngno

Unp'yŏngno

Kayaro

Yonhūro

Ūijiro

Sŏgangno

Kyŏngbokkung Palace
and National
Folklore Museum

National Museum of Korea
(Former Capitol)

Ch'angdŏkkung Palace
and Secret Garden

Ch'anggyŏnggung Palace

Pomunsa
Temple

Pugaksangil

Yukjokno

Insadong Antique and
Handicraft Market

US Embassy
Chogyesa Temple and
Buddhist Supply Shops

British Embassy
Tŏksugung Palace

Seoul Immigration Office

Seoul Metropolitan
Police Office

Seoul
Station

Chongmyo
Royal Shrine

Chongno

Tourism Information Centre

Airline Offices
(Westin Chosun Hotel)

Seoul Central Post Office

Myŏngdong

Namdaemun
South Gate and Market

Royal Asiatic
Society

Ch'aegyŏngūngno

T

(East

Ch'ŏngye

Ch'anggyŏnggung Palace

Olchiro

Taep'yŏngno

Namdaemun

Sogong no

Olchiro

Tŏegyero

Sinch'onno

To Kimpo Airport

Sŏgoro

Map oro

Seoul Tower
and Namsan
Park

Ch'ŏngp'a ro

Pang oro

Pang oro

Chungch'ungdan-gil

Taseno

Kangbyŏnno

Yŏngchoro

Sŏgangno

Yukido Plaza

63 Dae Han Life Insurance
Building and Yŏ'ŭido

It'aewŏn

Sobinggoro

HAN GANG
(RIVER)

Kongbyŏnno

Olympic daero

Hyŏnch'ungno

Taedaergno

Sampodogangnl

Shinbanp oro

Sap yŏngno

Sap yŏngno

Pang oro

Chamwon

Uimdoro

Seoul Express
Bus Terminal

72

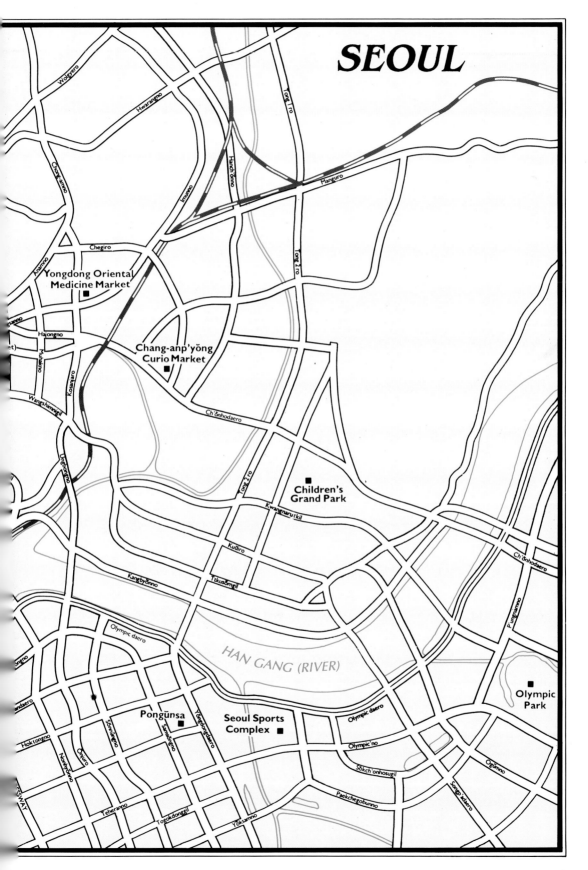

SEOUL

Yongdong Oriental
Medicine Market

Chang-anp'yŏng
Curio Market

Children's
Grand Park

HAN GANG (RIVER)

Olympic
Park

Pongŭnsa

Seoul Sports
Complex

Wolgyero

Hwarangno

Tong 1 ro

Imuno

Hanch'onno

Manguro

Chegiro

Chegiro

Tong 2 ro

Hajongno

Kosanro

Ch'ŏnhodaero

Wangshimnigil

Kwangnaru kil

Tong 2 ro

Ch'ŏnhodaero

Kuŭiro

Kangbyŏnno

Ttuksŏmgil

Olympic daero

P'ungnamno

Olympic daero

Olympic daero

Olympic'no

Sŏkch'onhosugil

Ch'ŏnhodaero

Ogŭmno

Songp'adaero

Songp'adaero

Hoktongno

Sŏnnŭngno

Naksŏngno

Ch'uro

Yŏngdongdaero

Samdaero

Paekchegobunno

Teheranno

Togokdonggil

Tŏksanno

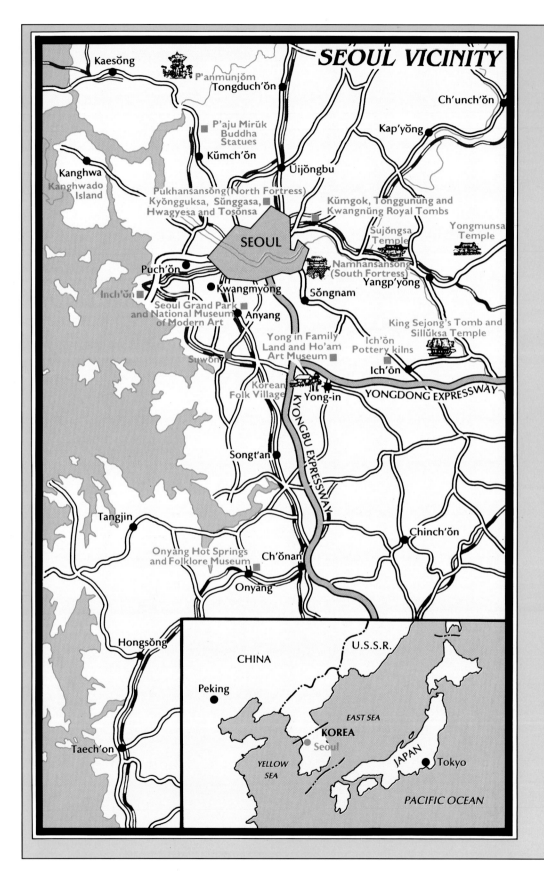

SEOUL VICINITY

Kaesŏng

P'anmunjŏm
Tongduch'ŏn

Ch'unch'ŏn

Kap'yŏng

P'aju Mirŭk
Buddha
Statues

Kŭmch'ŏn

Ŭijŏngbu

Kanghwa

Kanghwado
Island

Pukhansansŏng(North Fortress)
Kyŏngguksa, Sŭnggasa,
Hwagyesa and Tosŏnsa

Kŭmgok, Tonggunŭng and
Kwangnŭng Royal Tombs

Yongmunsa
Temple

Sujŏngsa
Temple

SEOUL

Puch'ŏn

Namhansansŏng
(South Fortress)

Kwangmyŏng

Yangp'yŏng

Sŏngnam

Inch'ŏn

Seoul Grand Park
and National Museum
of Modern Art

Anyang

King Sejong's Tomb and
Sillŭksa Temple

Yong in Family
Land and Ho'am
Art Museum

Ich'ŏn
Pottery kilns

Suwŏn

Ich'ŏn

Korean
Folk Village

Yong-in

YONGDONG EXPRESSWAY

Songt'an

KYONGBU EXPRESSWAY

Tangjin

Chinch'ŏn

Onyang Hot Springs
and Folklore Museum

Ch'ŏnan

Onyang

Hongsŏng

U.S.S.R.

CHINA

Peking

EAST SEA

KOREA

Seoul

YELLOW
SEA

JAPAN

Tokyo

Taech'ŏn

PACIFIC OCEAN

74

## Seoul Sidelights

**SOUL OF SEOUL.** Until 1948, when the Republic of Korea was founded, the official name for Seoul was Hansŏng-bu or simply Hanyang, a Chinese-derived word meaning "north of the Han River." For centuries the city had been unofficially called "Seoul," a pure Korean word derived from the ancient *sŏrabol* meaning "the center of everything." For most, Koreans, it had always been just that and Seoul eventually became the city's official name.

**ARTFUL TRANSACTION.** Seoul may be the only art capital in the world where paintings are sold by square measure like bolts of cloth or plots of land. Before a customer pays for a painting by a living Korean artist, the dealer counts up the number of postcard-sized squares that fit into the painting and multiplies that by the artist's standard rate. Never mind the quality of the work; if you're a big-time collector, it's size that counts.

**UNPLEASANT DREAMS.** Streetcars ran on the streets of Seoul from 1899 to 1968. On sultry summer nights Seoulites slept on the tracks, using the cool rails as pillows. The streetcars' last run was at 11:30 p.m. every day. One night the last car started late — after sleepers who thought the final car had passed had already bedded down for the night. The next morning, their bodies were found — minus the heads. After that incident, the city government issued an order forbidding anyone from sleeping on the rails. But people objected so vociferously that the decree was recalled. Thereafter, the city fathers always made sure the last streetcar ran on time.

**BACKS TO THE FUTURE.** The sexes are far from equal in this Confucian land where every person is supposed to know his or her place. But Korean women have come a long way. Until the opening of the Ehwa Institute (now Ewha Woman's University) in Seoul in 1886, Korea had no schools for girls. Even then, male teachers had to lecture behind a curtain lest they cast an eye upon their innocent students. The major breakthrough came in 1892. A male teacher of Chinese was allowed to lecture the girls without a curtain. But there was a catch: when the teacher entered the classroom, the girls would turn around and face the back of the room. The teacher in turn sat down — and faced the black-board in front of the room. At the sound of his discreet cough, the girls would turn towards the front again and the lesson began with the teacher lecturing the blackboard and the girls looking at the back of his head. Today at Ehwa, teaching conditions have normalized but men are still restricted in their access to the campus.

**CITY SYMBOLS.** Forsythia is the official flower of Seoul, ginko the official tree, and the magpie the official bird.

**ROYAL CONNECTION.** The first telephone was installed in Seoul in 1898. King Kojong, who reigned from 1850 to 1907 as Korea's first and last emperor (rather than king), placed the first call.

**DOG SOUP.** In 1884 Horace Allen, a missionary doctor, was treating Prince Min Yong-ik for wounds suffered in a clash with Japanese troops. The doctor discovered that palace attendants were feeding the prince dog soup in order to strengthen him. Concealing his repulsion, he told his royal patient that this was a unique way of taking revenge on his enemies — by eating them. He said that he had seen dogs devouring the corpses of dead Japanese lying on the streets outside the palace: thus, by eating the dogs, the prince was devouring his enemies, the good Dr. Allen explained. After hearing that news, the cooks switched to making the soup from beef and the corpses of the Japanese were removed and buried. The government has since outlawed dog soup, or *posint'ang*, but it's still surreptitiously eaten by Korean men who believe that it enhances their virility and mental facilities.

**SAGE CAMPUS.** Seoul claims the oldest campus in Korea, established in 1288 on the grounds of present-day Sungkyunkwan University. During the Yi Dynasty, this college also housed the city's main shrine to Confucius. Today, twice yearly in the spring and fall, the centuries-old ceremony of *sŏkchonje*, or Confucian rites, are held in the beautiful courtyard of the campus to honor the Great Sage and his disciples.

**GHOSTBUSTERS.** Ghosts have had an important influence on Seoul architecture. As every Korean knows, spirits travel from north to south and cannot turn corners easily. To prevent any wandering spirits from getting in and causing havoc, the people used to build their houses facing south. This accounts for the southerly orientation of many of Seoul's palaces, tombs and temples. After all, royalty and clergy had to suffer the whims of spirits just like everyone else. In fact, owners of upper-class structures who wanted to be doubly safe often placed a partition just inside the gate. Should any ghost careen off course and get through the gate, it would run smack into this barrier.

**FOOD FOR THOUGHT.** A Korean proverb says, "He who enjoys his food should never look over the kitchen wall." A king, according to legend, once peeked over the kitchen wall of his Seoul palace to check on his dinner. He saw a filthy kitchen maid carrying a pyramid of luscious persimmons out of the kitchen when a gust of wind blew dirt all over the fruit. Unperturbed, the maid carefully picked up each persimmon, licked it clean, reassembled the pyramid on a clean tray, then marched triumphantly towards the king's quarters.

**THE MISSING FLOOR.** The Chinese-derived Korean word for the number four, *sa*, is identical in pronunciation to the word for death. Consequently developers avoid designating a fourth floor in Seoul, much the way buildings in the West are often missing the 13th floor.

**CHRISTIAN STRONGHOLD.** Seoul has more than 4,500 churches, nearly one church for every 2,200 persons. Of the 10 largest church congregations in the world, Seoul has seven. The largest is the Full Gospel Central Church, claiming a membership of over 50,000 under the leadership of Reverend Cho Yong-gi. Each of the church's seven Sunday services accommodates more than 10,000 believers, beginning at 6:30 a.m. when they arrive aboard dozens of buses. Video screens are provided for those sitting far from the pulpit and there is simultaneous translation of the sermon into eight foreign languages.

**NOSE OMELETTE.** At the National Museum of Korea in Seoul, some of the stone Buddhas have no noses, not because the statues once stood outdoors and have weathered the ravages of time and climate, nor because of attacks by Muslim invaders who defaced religious images in India, China and Southeast Asia as incompatible with Islam. The missing noses are a result of the Korean greed for male offspring. The pressure to bear sons was so strong that desperate women embraced the folk belief that eating the powdered nose of a stone Buddha would enable them to conceive a boy. Thus, many sonless women stole into the night to chip off a bit of the Buddha's nose and grind it up for their next morning's breakfast.

**DON'T LOOK NOW.** Skyscrapers now abound in downtown Seoul but when Korea still had kings no building in Seoul was allowed to be taller than the royal residences because it was considered disrespectful for subjects to look down on their rulers. This practice had a resurrection of sorts for security reasons during the presidency of Park Chung-hee: buildings overlooking the Blue House were required to install smoked glass windows to obscure the view. The idea was abandoned when buildings climbed to even greater heights. Photographs of the compound are prohibited, however.

**SNOWBOUND.** Seoul may be the only city in the world where snow is shoveled into the street instead of out of it. After a blizzard, public works teams shovel snow off sidewalks and curbs into the pathway of oncoming vehicles on the theory that the vehicles will crush the snow until it's gone. Meanwhile, drive with caution and with snow tires.

**CHIMES OF CHONG-NO.** Downtown Seoul's Chong-no, which means Bell Street, is named after the great bell hanging at the intersection of Chong-no and Namdaemun-no. To signal the opening and closing of the city gates in the old days, the bell was rung 33 times each morning (for the 33 heavens of Buddhism) and 28 times each evening (for the 28 stars which determine man's fate). The evening bell was called Injŏng, Director of Man. At Injŏng those outside the city had to hurry back in or spend the night among bandits outside the walls. Those inside had to clear the streets. Surprisingly, usually only women were out at night. Modesty prevented ladies from appearing in public in broad daylight so they only ventured out under the cover of night to stretch their legs and visit female friends. Men found on the streets after dusk were arrested as suspected thieves. At midnight, even the women cleared the streets when the great bell was struck once.

**HOLIER THAN THOU.** During his visit to Seoul in 1984, Pope John Paul II canonized 103 Korean martyrs on Yŏ'iu-do Plaza. It was the largest single canonization service in Catholic history and the only one ever held outside of Rome.

**BLOOD BATH.** Most historical sites in Seoul have a story attached to them and Segŏm-jŏng, the Sword-washing Pavilion, is no exception. Located in a picturesque valley in hills behind the Kyŏngbok Palace, it has a blood-curdling history. The 15th king of the Yi Dynasty, Kwanghae Gun, presided over a reign of terror and murder from 1608 to 1623. Unable to bear his excesses any longer, a nephew named Injo and several other conspirators plotted to overthrow him. On their way to the coup d'etat they stopped by a stream in a small paper-making village to wash and sharpen their swords before the blood bath. In 1748, a pavilion was erected on the spot where Injo was thought to have lingered on his way to becoming the 16th king of the dynasty.

**LEG INSURANCE.** The Sup'yo-gyo, or Water Gauge Bridge, in Chang-h'ung-dan Park is now just another ornamental relic from the glorious reign of King Sejong (1418-50). For centuries, however, the bridge served the important function of forestalling floods. It had markers which measured the water level of the river that it spanned, the Ch'ŏnggye-ch'ŏn, on which many of Seoul's shops and houses were located. At the annual *Taeborum*, or First Full Moon Festival in February, the Sup'yo Bridge took on a romantic function. Koreans believed that by crossing a bridge on *Taeborum*, one would be protected from leg ailments for the rest of the year. (The Korean word for leg has the same sound as that for bridge.) The more times a person crossed the bridge, the more protection he received. The custom was popular among sheltered young ladies, for whom *Taeborum* was the only evening of the year when they were free to wander about outdoors in mixed company.

**POLITICAL PLURALISM.** After Japan surrendered at the end of World War II in August, 1945, the U.S. Army arrived to liberate Korea and set up a temporary military government. In 1946, it called on all political parties in Korea to be registered. The Army was mystified when 425 parties and social organizations filed the proper papers, claiming a collective membership of 52 million. The adult population of South Korea at that time was about 4.5 million, less than half that of Seoul alone today.

**PUSHING TOO HARD.** The pushing and shoving that occurs on the streets of Seoul is perplexing. Koreans historically are polite, gentle people. One old-timer traces the degeneration of public behavior to the Korean War. In 1950, when Communist North Korean troops swept down on Seoul, city residents were jammed up for days trying to escape across the single bridge over the Han River that could accommodate vehicle and pedestrian traffic. "The aggressive, pushy types scrambled ahead to safety south of the river" he says, "while gentlemen were trapped behind, some captured by the communists and taken north. Ever since, Seoulites feel they have to push, push, and push to survive."

**GINSENG** is the famed oriental medicinal root that is native to Korea. A shy plant that likes to find a shady spot in the high mountains, it has been cultivated in Korea for thousands of years. South Koreans today continue the practice of cultivating ginseng and it can be spotted in the countryside beneath rows of tiny thatch-like sheds. It is claimed to cure everything from sexual impotence to old age, when taken in regular doses over a long period. It is "yang," or hot, in the Korean scheme of medicine. Ginseng is prepared in powdered form to make a pleasant tea that is served with honey. It is also popular to put a whole root inside a small chicken, stuff it with rice and dates and boil it up. The most powerful roots are red ginseng. The good ones are rare, harder to find than truffles, and are like the Irish leprechaun's famed pot of gold to many poor farmers who occasionally stumbled across a prime root in the mountains and sell it for thousands of dollars!

## Seoul Tours

**ROYAL SEOUL**. Of all of the potential sight-seeing tours in Seoul, this is the most rewarding. The major palaces of Seoul, which have been preserved and restored, provide a unique glimpse into the greatness of Korea's political and cultural past, the highly-refined royal tradition of the Yi Dynasty. In the past, only a tiny, powerful elite was privileged to see and experience this dynastic heritage. Now everyone can marvel at it. Although this tour can be completed in one day, it's better to spread it out over several days to give yourself enough time to absorb the legacy of centuries of cultural development.

Begin the tour in front of the Tŏksu-gung Palace (**1**). South of you is the monumental Namdae-mun or Great South Gate (**2**), built in 1396 by more than 8,000 men as part of the old walled city of Seoul. To the north is the Kwanghwa-mun (**3**), the ancient entrance to the Kyŏngbok Palace (**4**), the former seat of government which dates back to the same year.

To the east, tucked between the Westin Chosun and the President Hotel, is the Altar of Heaven (**5**), built in 1897 when Korea declared itself an empire, as opposed to a mere kingdom, under the wing of China. In the Confucian scheme of things, only empires had the right to call on heaven from a specially-designed altar.

By now you should have your bearings. Enter the Tŏksu-gung, the Palace of Virtuous Longevity, built for Prince Wolson (1454–88) as a consolation prize for losing the throne to a younger brother. Several Western-style structures were added to the compound in the early 20th century, but many old-style buildings remain. The most notable is the Chunghwa-jŏn, or Hall of Central Harmony, an audience hall. The stone markers where officials once assembled according to their rank still line the pavement leading up to the hall. Pause at the statue of the most famous of all of Korea's rulers, King Sejong (1418–50), who invented the Korean script called *Han'gŭl*. Afterwards, view the Kwangmyŏng-mun, an open pavilion containing a water clock made in 1536, and the Hŭngch'ŏn-sa Bell, cast in 1461. Like almost all Yi Dynasty palaces, the Tŏksu-gung originally had a north–south orientation, but modern renovations relocated the main gate on the east side.

After you leave the Tŏksu-gung, turn left and walk up Sejong-no towards Kwanghwa-mun. For centuries, this ancient pathway felt the footsteps

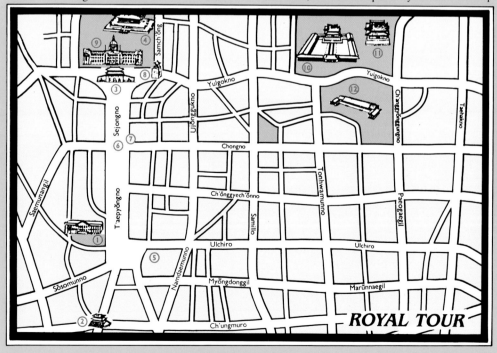

ROYAL TOUR

of royalty and commoner alike. The towering modern bronze statue (6) that faces south as you approach the large intersection is that of Admiral Yi Sun-shin (1545–98), the national hero who invented the turtle-shelled, turtle-shaped ships that repelled the Japanese navy during the Hideyoshi invasions. Then enter the underground walkway at the corner. Cross the street diagonally and emerge on the corner of the Pigak (7), a pavilion erected to King Kojong in 1902.

Keep going north past the American Embassy and continue until you can see that the Kwanghwa-mun is flanked by a pair of fierce-looking stone *haet'ae* statues whose function was to protect the Kyŏngbok Palace by eating fire and destroying evil. Turn the corner and use the underpass to cross the street. Emerging on the southeast corner of the Kyŏngbok-kung, you can see the Tongsipja-gak (8), a 1395 tower that was once attached to the palace wall. From here head for the east entrance into the Kyŏngbok-kung or detour into the National Museum of Korea (9), the former colonial capitol built by the Japanese from 1916–26.

The Kyŏngbok-kung, or Palace of Shining Happiness, was constructed by T'aejo, the first king of the Yi Dynasty. It was largely destroyed in 1592 during the Hideyoshi invasions from Japan. Some of the main buildings have been restored to their former glory. There is much to see and experience in this old palace, all well-documented with detailed maps and commentaries posted around the compound. Don't miss the gorgeous Hyangwŏn-jŏng, a hexagonal pavilion set in the middle of a lotus pond, or the Kyŏnghoe-ru, a royal banquet pavilion that could accommodate up to 100 guests. Finally, take a look into the National Folklore Museum, which contains excellent life-sized dioramas depicting all aspects of traditional Korean life during the Yi Dynasty.

On leaving the Kyŏngbok-kung, retrace your steps to the corner, proceed east along Yulgok-no to the Ch'angdŏk Palace and the Piwon or Secret Garden (10). Because members of the royal family still live on the premises, you can only enter the Ch'angdŏk-kung on guided tours. English tours begin daily at 11:30 in the morning and 1:30 and 3:30 in the afternoon.

The guided tour of the Ch'angdŏk-kung, or Palace of Illustrious Virtue, and the Secret Garden takes approximately one and a half hours. The palace, built in 1394 by King T'aejo, served as the official residence of the Yi kings from the 17th century to the mid-19th century. Behind the palace is the Secret Garden, a former royal refuge and recreational area. Once populated by deer, the garden is beautifully-landscaped, harmonizing streams, ponds, springs and ornate pavilions with a great variety of native and imported trees. Within the garden is the unpainted Yŏn'gyŏng-dang, a commoner's residence to which the royal family retreated when they wanted to relax by pretending to be ordinary people. If you want to stay forever young, be sure to walk through the Pullo-mun, or Gate of No Aging, which was carved from a solid piece of stone.

The Ch'anggyŏng Palace (11) and the Chong-myo Royal Shrine (12), the last two stops on the tour, are easy to find. Exit the Ch'angdŏk-kung, turn left and continue east, then head north along the wall for 20 minutes until you come to the entrance to the Ch'anggyŏng-gung.

Built in 1419 by King Sejong for his retired father, King T'aejong, the Ch'anggyŏng-gung, or Palace of Glorious Blessing, and the Chong-myo Royal Shrine are connected by a bridge over Yulgok-no. The Japanese constructed the street to separate the palace from its spiritual source, the shrine. The colonialists also relegated the palace to the status of a park and located a zoo there. The zoo has been moved to the Seoul Grand Park and some of the palace buildings have been restored. Behind the halls and palace buildings are a lake and a colonial *fin de siècle* greenhouse containing a great variety of native Korean plants. The east–west orientation of the Ch'anggyŏng-gung is unusual in that it follows a Koryŏ rather than Yi Dynasty pattern, which is north–south.

Cross the bridge over Yulgok-no and enter the grounds of the Chong-myo, the royal shrine of the kings and queens of the Yi Dynasty, first erected in 1396. Also enshrined here are the ancestral spirit tablets of those who were given the title of king and queen posthumously. On the first Sunday in May every year, the descendants of the Yi Dynasty hold a grand ceremony here to honor their royal ancestors. The rites are open to the public.

From the Chong-myo, it's an easy walk to Insa-dong. In fact, getting anywhere on foot may prove faster than trying to move around by car or taxi. Car ownership is projected to increase 250 per cent between 1986 and 1990. Because of the crush, the transport ministry estimates that the average vehicle speed in rush hour is only 19 kph.

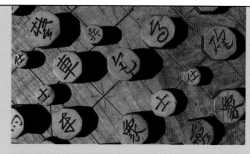

**INSA-DONG ANTIQUES AND HANDI-CRAFTS.** Unless you are pressed for time, avoid shopping for antiques, handicrafts and souvenirs in hotel shops. With few exceptions, prices are much inflated. Department stores and underground shopping arcades charge fair prices, but are rather sterile and chaotic places to shop. It'ae-wŏn offers the best bargains, but quality and taste are not consistently high. That leaves Insa-dong for those seeking to bring home something tasteful and enduring from South Korea. Even if you are not interested in souvenirs, Insa-dong is a good place to get a "hands-on" experience of Korea's rich artistic and cultural heritage.

Because many goods in Insa-dong are handmade, prices may seem high. But gentle bargaining will get you a 10-15% discount, more if it's an antique, at some shops. Allow about two hours for this tour, longer if you plan to do some serious buying. Most shopkeepers speak some English and Japanese.

The Doriking Japanese Restaurant (1) specializes in grilled meats, seafood, mushrooms and ginko nuts on bamboo skewers and clay-pot rice casseroles. It's a perfect spot for a beer and conversation before you start shopping. Tong Moon Kwan (2) deals in rare Korean books. Owner Ree Gyum Ro has been in business since 1934 and delights in tracking down old or obscure Korean books and maps.

The Royang Tearoom (3) above the barber shop serves only green tea, about 20 varieties of it. A popular hangout for Zen monks, artists, musicians and students, it stages free cultural performances or art lessons every last Wednesday of the month. For W1,000, owner Kang Po-mi will personally brew and serve you a fresh pot of delicious Korean green tea served with crackers. Regular customers have tea cups named after them.

Dong Mun Dang (4) offers high-class Korean screens, folk and classical paintings for the serious collector. Prices are high but generally commensurate with the level of taste and authenticity. Dadoga Ceramics (5) offers handmade celadons, *punchong* wares and tea sets. It is a favorite of Japanese tourists who have to pay much more for similar items back home.

Nine different kinds of the famous dance masks of Hahoe Village are sold at the Talbang Shop (6). Hahoe is a remote community in Southeast Korea where, like the Amish group of the United States' Midwest, the resi-

**SHOPPING TOUR**

dents have steadfastly refused to change their traditional way of life.

Yedang (7) offers modern ceramics made by a young potters' cooperative. If you want to see what Korean yuppies put on the table, this is it. Prices are comparable to similar wares overseas. Dohansa (8) features Korean celadons and tea bowls produced by famous potters. Wooden packing boxes are made to order.

The Yong Bin Garden Restaurant (9) is a good place to take the kids for a mid-shopping meal, or, if you work in Seoul, the office staff for lunch. *Pulgogi* and *kalbi* are served in a traditional Korean setting. The three-story Kwanhun Art Gallery (10) exhibits works by young artists. The outdoor area is used for sculpture.

The Kyung-in Museum and Tearoom (11) was formerly one of the "eight great residences of Seoul." Park Yong-hyo, a member of the royal family and an anti-Japanese revolutionary made his home here. Go Bo Dang (12) sells old Korean jewelry, accessories and small antiques. Colorful beads from 7th to 8th century Korean tombs for making that conversation-piece necklace can also be purchased here.

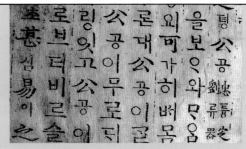

The small Orchid Shop (13) carries some rare specimens as well as all the paraphernalia needed to raise the delicate Korean orchid. Do Ok Sa Ceramics (14) is excellent for good quality Korean ceramics at very reasonable prices. They make wooden packing boxes and ship overseas. Hengp'o Lacquerwares (15) offers beautiful food trays, bowls and gift items at fair prices. For old Korean coins and stamps step into Kŭmhwa-sa Coin Shop (16); while the Tong-in Store (17) is a one-stop shopping center for Korean antiques, crafts and souvenirs. It has been in business for 60 years and has several floors selling antique chests and porcelains, folk art, furniture reproductions, Korean bedding, contemporary crafts and gift items. It's a good place to buy handicrafts for the folks back home.

Sanch'on Restaurant (18) is a vegetarian gourmet's delight tucked away in a Korean-style house. Traditional music and dance are performed at dinner, which makes this a good place to take a date. Set meals begin at W5,000.

The Gold House Antiques (19) was once owned by Chong Hae-sok, a prominent dealer who was murdered along with his wife and driver during the 1970s antique boom. The crime was never solved. The store has several floors of gold art, screens, chests, ceramics, old paintings and maps. Be sure to bargain; prices start high.

Chonggak Gallery (20) offers traditional ink paintings, fans and watercolors at good prices. Buy that oriental scroll you've always wanted here. Adang Coffee House (21), decorated in rustic Korean style, brews up a good cup of coffee and assorted Korean teas. Sun Gallery (22) exhibits works by well-known contemporary Korean artists. Owner Kim Chang-shil is the chairman of the Gallery Association.

The Human Cultural Assets Handicraft Gallery (23) sells kites, macrame, masks, fans, lacquer and woodcrafts made by artisans who are recognized by the government for their efforts to preserve Korea's traditional crafts. Mass-produced souvenirs and Olympics merchandise are also marketed at this commercial gallery.

Two well-known shops, the Wha-An (24), which specializes in fine reproduction furniture (see the feature "Antiques to Order"), and the Mee Gallery (25), which exhibits works by famous contemporary artists, are in the basement arcade of the Hanaro Christian Building. Choung Ahn Antiques (26) and the four antique shops next to it on the same side of the street have interesting old pieces at somewhat inflated prices. Make a counter offer if you are interested in something. Kyŏng-il Paper Shop (27) has an excellent selection of painting brushes, hand-made paper, kites, paper fans and umbrellas at reasonable prices. Taxis are easy to catch from this intersection, but most downtown hotels are only a 15-minute walk away.

**OLD RESIDENTIAL NEIGHBORHOODS.** The tourist brochures unfailingly bill Seoul as a city of contrasts in which the traditional and the modern coexist in cozy harmony. This is unabashed advertising hype. Except for the five royal palaces and gardens, and a dozen or so gates, walls and bridges, most of ancient Seoul was leveled during the Korean War. What stands today is a sprawling metropolis of drab but friendly two- and three-story concrete or brick-faced storefronts and residences. These hastily-built post-war structures are quickly giving way to skyscrapers and tall apartment blocks. There is, however, one section of town which retains the flavor of old Seoul.

Located between the Kyŏngbok-kung and the Secret Garden, and designated a preservation zone for Korean-style houses, the area contains about 600 examples of the traditional U-shaped middle-class Korean house architecture, as well as several large aristocratic mansions. Allow yourself a leisurely two hours to enjoy the area's narrow, winding lanes, tile-roofed houses, quaint Mom and Pop shops, and children hamming it up for your camera.

The Hyundai Art Gallery and adjacent Jun Coffee Shop (1) is the oldest commercial gallery in Korea and a very popular rendezvous point for chic Seoulites. It exhibits contemporary works by medium-priced artists and introduces overseas Korean artists to the local market.

The Korea Traditional Clothes Association (2) is one of the most prestigious makers of *hanbok*, the traditional Korean dress. Owner Lee Rhea Za has been in business for 23 years and charges W150,0000 to W350,000 for a *hanbok*. Her standards are exacting. If you want a *hanbok* only for fun, get one made up for half the price at the East Gate Market.

Where the road forks, bear right. The left fork leads to the Ch'ongwa-dae (3), the Blue House, the official residence of the President of the Republic of Korea. It takes its name from the cobalt tiles on the roof — about all that most people ever see of the place. In 1974, North Korean commandos shot their way up to the estate using another approach in a daring but

failed attempt to assassinate former president Park Chung-hee.

Just before the sidewalk elevates above street level is an antique shop (4) owned by Mrs Kim Min-yea. She sells Korean antique furniture and folk art. The best items are kept upstairs and usually can be seen only by appointment. At the other end of the elevated sidewalk, glance across the street at the heavily-guarded Prime Minister's residence (5), built in the massive Korean-Western style favored by the country's ruling elite and many wealthy tycoons.

Yong Soo San Restaurant (6) specializes in royal Korean cuisine and is one of the favorite haunts of Seoul's beau monde. For refreshment, try the tiny old tea room (7) opposite the Yong Soo San. Here you can sample traditional Korean teas, all medicinal. Besides the old standby, *insam-cha* or ginseng, there is *saenggang-cha*, a ginger and herb tea, and *yuja-cha*, a citron and honey tea. The herbs for the teas are displayed in the window. never mind the strange tastes: they're all good for you!

Beyond the tea room, the road forks again. Keep heading straight towards the Samch'ŏng Tunnel if you want to see Chibo-sa (8), a small but non-touristy Buddhist temple. Or take a sharp right towards Samch'ŏng Park, passing an alley leading to the unmarked (in English) Nam Moon Korean Restaurant (9). The menu is similar to the one at the Yong Soò San, but the prices and decor are fancier. It's a popular spot for ladies' luncheons. Meals start at W10,000 per head and are worth the price.

Samch'ŏng Park (10) encompasses 15,000 square meters and dates to the early days of the Yi Dynasty when Confucian offerings to heaven were made here. The water from the Brother's Well is considered holy and still pure enough to drink. Old men come here to dream about immortality. Pathways are fenced on both sides to guard military installations on the hillside.

When you exit the park, head up to the Board of Audit (11), where you can catch a cool breeze and a panoramic view of Seoul. Then cross the street, bear left and take the road that goes downhill. Seoul Tower is straight ahead. The street is lined with the modern estates of Seoul's upper class. Behind them are whole blocks of old Korean houses, the heart of this tour.

The alley opposite the Saudi Arabia Residence (12) leads into the old neighborhood of Kahoe-dong (13), which was geomantically one of the most auspicious places to live in Seoul. During the Yi Dynasty, it was occupied exclusively by nobility. Other alleys further down the road lead to the pre-war neighborhoods of Kye-dong (14) and Anguk-dong (15) where the old family estate of former president Yun Po-son is located.

Your walk ends at the Anguk Subway Station (16), where it's easy to catch a taxi or train. Or enter the subway and rest your weary feet at the Paris Croissant Coffee Shop. Treat yourself to a genuine all-American Baskin Robbins ice cream cone or double-scoop chocolate soda here.

**MYŎNG-DONG FOOD TOUR.** Seoul's version of Tokyo's famous Ginza, Myŏng-dong, has been the epicenter of haute coutre and entertainment since early in the 20th century when Japanese merchants came to set up shops selling high-class consumer items and the Chinese opened eating places and small trading posts that sold silks and dry goods. After liberation from the Japanese in 1945, Myŏng-dong went avant garde and became a magnet for university students, patriots, artists and poets. They patronized its stylish cafes which served Western beverages to the high-brow sound of classical music.

Today, Myŏng-dong is more high fashion and

WALKING TOUR

Samch'ŏng Tunnel — Mountains

Samch'ŏng Park

Kahoe-dong

Sŏgyŏk Police Station

Entrance to Kyŏngbokkung

Kye-dong

Anguk-dong

Yulgokno — Secret Garden

Korea Times Building

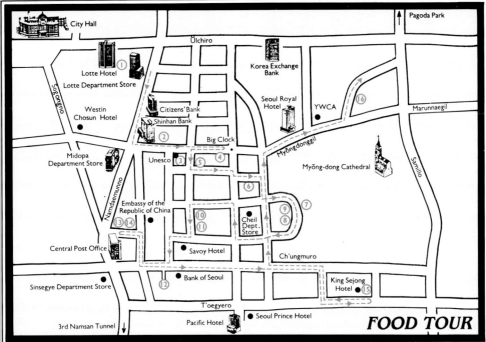

## FOOD TOUR

(Map labels:)

City Hall
Pagoda Park
Ŭlchiro
Korea Exchange Bank
Lotte Hotel
Lotte Department Store
Sogongno
Westin Chosun Hotel
Citizens' Bank
Shinhan Bank
Seoul Royal Hotel
YWCA
Marunnaegil
Big Clock
Midopa Department Store
Unesco
Myŏngdonggil
Myŏng-dong Cathedral
Samillo
Namdaemunno
Embassy of the Republic of China
Cheil Dept. Store
Central Post Office
Savoy Hotel
Ch'ungmuro
Sinsegye Department Store
Bank of Seoul
King Sejong Hotel
T'oegyero
3rd Namsan Tunnel
Pacific Hotel
Seoul Prince Hotel

---

finance than night life. Most clubs have followed the exodus of Seoul's population south of the Han River and moved to Pangbae-dong and Apkujŏng-dong. However, there are still a number of good restaurants in Myŏng-dong that do a brisk day-time business and stay open at night to catch the stray office worker or adventurous tourist. Some of these are tiny hole-in-the-wall gems; others are hard-to-miss. Korean food dominates. No tipping, please.

The Restaurant Row (1), located on the 9th and 10th floor of the Lotte Department Store, houses about 25 establishments that should suit every taste and budget. Each of these establishments displays plastic mock-ups of its dishes along with their prices (ranging from W1,000 to W6,000) in the window. The Row is efficient and clean, and is an excellent introduction to Seoul food.

The alley across the street from Midopa Department Store leads to central Myŏng-dong. On your left, squeezed between the Gucci Shop and a popular Japanese-style restaurant is the small family-owned Ch'ui Ch'on Ru Mandu Restaurant (2) which makes the best Chinese dumplings in town; prices range from W1,000 to W1,800. Order them fried (*yaki mandu*), boiled (*mul mandu*) or steamed (*tong mandu*) to eat on the premises or boxed for take-out. The owners, who speak Mandarin, have been turning out dumplings in the same spot for three generations to the delight of locals and tourists.

For the budget traveler who wants to sample Korean-style Western food, there's the no-frills Yech'an (3) in the basement of the UNESCO Building. The speciality of the house is pizza but you can get everything from light breakfasts to continental dinners. Prices are W3,000–W6,000. In the ugly five-story building next to the police station, you'll find the the Han Il Kwan (4), a large, popular Korean restaurant that has been in business for more than 50 years. It serves excellent beef and noodle dishes; service is prompt and friendly: W,2000–W20,000.

At the other end of the alley between the police station and the Han Il Kwan is the second-story Paekche Samgyaet'ang Restaurant (5). *Samgyaet'ang* is Ginseng Chicken Casserole in less tongue-twisting parlance, a bland but nutritious one-dish meal in which a small chicken is stuffed with rice, dates, chestnuts, garlic and ginseng root, then cooked in its own broth in a

83

clay pot until tender. It makes a great restorative for jet lag and general lack of stamina.

The narrow Fish and Seafood Alley (6), just opposite the Yves Saint-Laurent Shop, is one of the few lanes in the area that retain the color of Myŏng-dong in the "good old days" before gentrification. As you walk down the short alley, the sight of impeccably fresh seafood displayed on ice in glass greets you, as do the welcoming shouts of the proprietors. A meal costs W1,500 to W5,000, but negotiate the price of your catch before sitting down.

Take a right when you emerge from the Fish and Seafood Alley, then an immediate left into a U-shaped lane. You should be able to find a good place to dine among several reputable restaurants here. The well-appointed Sinjong (7) specializes in teppenyaki (sliced grilled beef) and Genghis Khan in steamboat or hot pot, but simple noodle dishes are also available for W1,500–W5,000. A little further down is a good Japanese-style restaurant (8), while across the way is the Hallyosudo Grilled Fish Restaurant (9), which serves the best salt-water fish in town for prices ranging W1,500–W3,000.

The basement Dull-Dull Western-style Restaurant (10) lives up to its great-great name and is a must-see: the all-black decor can only be described as industrial modern. Each party is ushered into a private booth enclosed on all sides by walls. It's a good place for coffee and conversation. Prices: W2,500–W3,000. Further down Dull-Dull is Ie Hak (11), an established Korean restaurant specializing in beef dishes and Koreanized Japanese food. Private ondol-floor rooms are available on the 2nd and 3rd floors.

Next to the Bank of Seoul branch is a dead-end lane where you'll find the Chonju Pibim-pap Restaurant (12). Pibim-pap is a one-dish meal in which thinly-sliced meat, vegetables and beef are served over a bed of rice. Spoon off the glob of hot sauce if you don't want to set your tongue on fire.

There's no place downtown for an authentic Chinese meal. However, the 1,000 Chinese residents living near the Embassy of the Republic of China sometimes frequent the second-story Kui Bin Restaurant (13) just outside the embassy's gate. Prices are in the W2,000–W8,000 range. The Dohyangchun Chinese Bakery (14) at street level is excellent for traditional Chinese sweets made from scratch.

The locals claim that the most authentic Korean buffet is at the Unhasu Restaurant (15)

on the fourth floor of the King Sejong Hotel, which offers all you can eat from dishes representing all of Korea for W15,000. Profits from the restaurant support Sejong University.

To begin or top off your evening like the Koreans do, take a stroll down Suljip Golmok, Wine House Alley (16), and pop into one of the many inexpensive drinking houses that serve soju (refined rice wine), makkŏlli (fermented rice wine), draft beer or Western liquor. Drinks come with anju appetizers of peanuts, dried squid, scallion cakes, meat patties, sausage, clams and oysters in chili sauce. Bon appétit, or more appropriately, mani chapsu-seyo, as Koreans say, before digging in.

SUBURBAN LINE TOUR. Northern Seoul is ringed with craggy mountains that have been important to the city's defense. This train ride takes you to some of the historical and scenic spots that skirt those massifs. The Kyowoe-sŏn, or Suburban Line, leaves Seoul Station and arrives an hour and a half later in Ŭijŏngbu, a satellite city, 65 kilometers northeast of Seoul. En route you will pass college campuses, residential communities, cottage industries, rice paddies, farm villages and forested hills. There are 14 stops on the line; watch for the following:
— Sinch'on, where the train stops minutes after departure from Seoul. It is the site of the prestigious Ewha Woman's University and Yonsei University. If you experience a burning sensation in your eyes at this station, it's probably tear-gas wafting in from one of the frequent campus protest demonstrations.
— Nŭnggok, some 16 kilometers from Seoul, the site of the Haengju Mountain Fortress. Situated strategically over the Han River, it witnessed one of the bloodiest battles in Korean history. General Kwŏn Yul defeated 30,000 Japanese troops during the Hideyoshi invasions of the late 16th century.
— Pyŏkche, in the heart of the farm and orchard area. Four stops after Nŭnggok, it is noted for its open-air kalbi and pulgogi or, for the more adventurous, wild boar and quail restaurants. At the village of Koyang-gun lies the tomb of General Ch'oe Yŏng, a powerful figure during the last days of the Koryŏ Dynasty (918–1392). He was killed by Yi Song-gye, the founder of the succeeding Yi Dynasty.
— Illyŏng, a family recreation area known for its freshwater fish restaurants, strawberry farms and camp ground beneath Mt. Nogo.
— Sŏngch'u, a farming area that doubles as a

weekend playground for Seoulites. Facilities include fishing farms, archery ranges, golf courses, camp grounds and restaurants.

**Ŭijŏngbu** is the end of the line but the starting point for day hikes up Surak-san and Tobong-san, where the temple sites of Ssangyong-sa, Mangowol-sa and Hweryŏng-sa are located.

A one-way ticket on the Kyowoe-sŏn costs W500. Trains leave from the west end of Seoul Station daily at 6:10 a.m., 2:15 p.m., and 6:25 p.m. and return from Ŭijŏngbu at 6:56 a.m.,

10:58 a.m. and 7:00 p.m. Extra trains are added on Sundays. Public buses run from Ŭijŏngbu to Seoul every 5 minutes and takes less than an hour.

**RURAL KOREA ON THE NARROW GAUGE RAIL.** This rigorous day-trip into rural Korea aboard the Suwŏn–Inch'ŏn narrow gauge rail is strictly for the hardy and adventurous. Don't worry about the potential confusion of navigating your way out of town by subway, rail, bus and taxi. It's worth the trouble. You will experience the tempo and color of ordinary

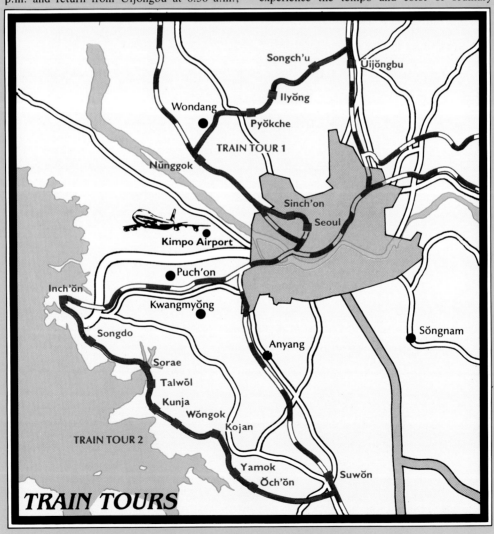

*TRAIN TOURS*

Korean life and feel as though you have finally arrived at the true heartland of Korea. It's best to begin the tour by 8 a.m., before the rush hour. To make the going easier, have your hotel write all Korean words and place names out in *Han'gŭl*, or Korean script.

Go to the subway at City Hall and buy a ticket on the #1 line to Suwŏn (W200). The ride is a 50-minute cruise through the bedroom communities of southern Seoul, with miles of high-rise apartment complexes.

At Suwŏn, walk out of the subway and into the Suwŏn Train Station next-door. At the information booth, confirm the departure time of the Suin-sŏn, or *hyopgye-sŏn* (narrow gauge line) from Suwŏn to Inch'ŏn. It should set out at 1:30 p.m. with tickets going on sale at 12:40. That gives you about three hours for sightseeing and lunch in Suwŏn.

**Historical Suwŏn** is an 18th-century walled city built by King Chongjo, who planned to relocate the capital there from Seoul so he could be near his father's grave. The move never materialized, however, and most of Suwŏn's old architecture has disappeared. About five kilometers of the old city walls and gates were restored in the 1970s. To see them, take a taxi outside the Suwŏn Train Station to Nam-mun, or the South Gate. Follow the wall from the gate as far as you want. There will be photo opportunities at the North Gate, West Gate, and on top of several fire beacons and pavilions.

Return to the South Gate at about noon and ask for the alley of *kalbi jip* (beef ribs restaurants). It is near the gate's taxi stand. In the 1960s the late president Park Chung-hee, who loved going out "among the people," patronized a *kalbi* restaurant in this alley. Since then, no visitor leaves Suwŏn without a meal of *kalbi* or *kalbi-tang* (beef rib soup with rice). Suwŏn *kalbi* houses use only the choicest Korean ribs; the servings are hefty but a bit pricey at W8,000 per person. The hearty beef rib soup is a bargain, though, at W2,000 for a large bowl with a large helping of *kimch'i* on the side.

Taxi back to Suwŏn Train Station at 1 p.m., then buy a ticket to Inch'ŏn on the Suin-sŏn at window #8. When you give your ticket to the conductor, ask him to escort you to the right platform to avoid losing your way.

After departure, the toy-like three-car Suin-sŏn bumps through town, wafts through the Suwŏn dump, and soon chugs its way through Korean farmland. You'll pass picturesque paddy fields, thatched farmhouses, women weeding vegetable plots, men transporting A-frames on their backs, cattle farms and waving school children. You'll also see ugly industrial towns, superhighways, salt flats and barbed-wire fences designed to keep North Korean agents from infiltrating through the Inch'ŏn coastline.

The 50-kilometer ride takes 1½ hours and makes stops at Ŏch'ŏn, Yamok, Kojan, Wŏn-gok, Kunja, Talwŏl, Sorae and Songdo. You can get off at Songdo, the last stop, and take a taxi to Dong Inch'ŏn Yŏk (East Inch'ŏn Station) to catch the #1 subway line back to City Hall in Seoul. But it's more fun to get off at **Sorae**, a small fishing village on the outskirts of Inch'ŏn. The coast has tidal fluctuations of 28 feet, one of the largest in the world. When the tide is out at Sorae, you can see miles of muddy flats and no fishing boats in sight. They are out at sea and have to wait until the tide comes in before returning home.

To get back to Seoul from Sorae, take the *si-nae* (city) bus to East Inch'ŏn Station and catch the subway. Or, if you still have the energy, you can take a taxi from the East Inch'ŏn Station to points of interest in **Inch'ŏn city,** the second largest port in South Korea after Pusan. They include: Chinatown, which retains some interesting early 20th-century Chinese architecture; Inch'ŏn City Museum; and the Foreigner's Cemetery.

Perhaps the most moving point of interest, at least for visiting Americans, is Freedom Park. The park commemorates General Douglas MacArthur's surprise landing at Inch'ŏn on September 15, 1950, a tactical move that changed the course of the Korean War and, of course, South Korea's history. MacArthur actually confronted and outflanked the North Korean invaders on nearby Green Beach. Still, the brutal war persisted until an armistice was signed on July, 1953; it had lasted three years and cost 4 million lives, including the loss of more than 33,000 American soldiers.

After the war, an oil refinery and iron, steel and glass factories were built in Inch'ŏn. Today it has become a thriving city in its own right with a population of more than one million. Other attractions in Inch'ŏn include the beach-side casino resort at the Olympos Hotel. Sun-worshippers will find that the best beaches near Seoul are on the islands, Song-do and Palmi-do just offshore from Inch'ŏn.

## Off the Beaten Track

**SPECIALTY MARKETS.** You'll get jostled and bumped and you must guard your wallet from overzealous shopkeepers and the occasional pickpocket, but a journey into one of Seoul's many wholesale markets is well worth the hassles. Prices are 10 to 30 per cent less than department stores and ordinary retail shops, even cheaper if you haggle.

The market at **Namdae-mun**, the **South Gate**, has been doing business this way since the end of the Koryŏ Dynasty (918–1392). The wholesale emporium of over 8,000 shops specializes in ready-made clothing, fashion accessories and jewelry, chinaware, silk flowers, lacquerwares, handicrafts and camping and mountaineering supplies. It is located at the City Hall stop on the #1 and #2 subway lines.

The market at **Tongdae-mun**, the **East Gate**, spans several square miles from Chong-no 6-ga to Ch'ŏnggyech'ŏn 4-ga. This area has been a marketplace since the beginning of the Yi Dynasty (1392–1910). Specialized buildings sell Korean silks and satins, fabrics for clothing and draperies, notions and buttons, Korean bedding, kitchen utensils, handicrafts, athletic and sporting goods. The Hŭng-in, Tŏgun, Cheil Pyŏnghwa, and Kwangh'ŭi wholesale marts behind the stadium carry ready-made clothing for the entire family in the latest export styles and sizes.

**Seun Arcade**, the "Electronics Market," is a paradise for the electronics buff or computer whiz. Everything from IBM compatible software to a spare part for that old stereo can be found in this maze of shops between Chong-no 4-ga and T'oegye-ro 4-ga. The whole complex was scheduled for removal to the site of the Yongsan Vegetable and Fruit Market in 1987. At the Chong-no 3-ga, stop on the #1 subway line.

The **Sŏch'o-dong Flower Market** is a great place to smell the flowers and take pretty pictures. Located behind the Seoul Express Bus Terminal, south of the Han River, it can be reached aboard the #3 subway line.

**Chang-anp'yŏng Antique Market** came into being because of the high rents in Insa-dong and urban renewal projects in the Tongdae-mun and Hwanghak-dong markets that forced many established dealers to relocate here in the early 1980s. The selection is vast and the prices excellent if you bargain. The market is located near the Kimil Gymnasium on Ch'ŏnhodae-ro Street in the direction of the Sheraton Walker Hill Hotel, so ask your concierge to provide you with taxi directions.

**"The Hwanghak-dong Flea Market"** is known as a poor man's antique market. The funky shops and stalls beneath apartments #15, 16, 17 and 18 at Ch'ŏnggyech'ŏn-no 8-ga feature collectibles, as well as some used appliances. You will find old earthen jars and porcelains, farm implements from bygone eras, window and door frames from traditional houses, gramophones, bronze Buddhas, stone grandfathers from Cheju Island, out-of-print books and maps, and Japanese period antiques. One long-established shop serves as Seoul's clearing house for the repair and resale of Japanese period wind-up pendulum clocks. Exit at the Tongdae-mun stop on the #1 and #4 subway lines.

For a fascinating alley of old-world apothecary shops selling *hanyak*, or Oriental medicine, try the **Kyong-dong Oriental Medicine Market**. The smells are pungent and the sights exotic. An adjacent alley has a wholesale spice, chili pepper and garlic market. Take the #1 subway line to the Chegi stop.

**Chungbu Dried Fish Market** is an unhurried, old-time wholesale market for dried marine products and special foods used for ancestor worship and rituals such as the 60th birthday feast, called *hwangap*. Get off the #2 subway at Ŭlchi-ro 4-ga.

The many small dining places inside the wholesale **Noryangjin Fresh Fish Market** have the freshest *sashimi* in Seoul. About 60 species of fresh fish from ports all over Korea are auctioned off here every morning between 4:30 a.m. and 8 a.m. The market stays open until sunset for the general public. It is at the Noryangjin stop on the #1 subway line.

**FINISHING SCHOOL.** Yejiwon, the Etiquette Institute, is the place to go to learn the proper way to take Korean tea or make a traditional bow before the elders. Short-term lessons on Korean social graces, traditional weddings, calligraphy, rice-cake and *kimch'i* making are regularly scheduled. Call 743-4731 for more information.

**BUDDHIST TEMPLES.** Because of the pro-Confucian bias of the Yi Dynasty, no important Buddhist temples survive within the city walls. Chogye-sa, the headquarters for celibate monks in downtown Seoul, was founded after the the Yi Dynasty had collapsed in 1910. Large Seoul temples with a long history like Pŏngwon-sa, headquarters for married monks near Yonsei University; Pomun-sa, a sprawling nunnery near Korea University; and Pongŭn-sa, a large temple complex near the KOEX Center south of the Han River, were all located outside the walls of the ancient city. Further out on the scenic slopes of Pukhan-san are the old temple sites of Kyŏngguk-sa above Kook Min University, Sŭngga-sa above the Kugi Tunnel, and Tosŏn-sa and Hwagye-sa near U'i-dong. Taxi drivers generally know the temples or the footpaths that lead to them and will be happy to take you.

**SHAMAN SHRINES.** Despite centuries of suppression, first by Buddhists then by Confucianists, Shamanism is still widely-practiced in Korea. This

ancient form of worship considers mountains to be sacred and two popular peaks in Seoul for Shaman *kut*, or rituals, are Samkak-san in Tobong-gu and Inwang-san in Sodaemun-gu, above the Independence Gate. Inwang-san has the Kuksa-dang, a historical shrine erected for the protection and prosperity of the nation, the Sŏn-pawi rocks where women go to pray for offspring, and a cluster of temples where private *kut* can often be observed. Take the #3 subway line to the Tongnimmun (Independence Gate) stop.

**GRAVE PICNICS.** At the turn of the century, Western residents of Seoul often packed an elegant picnic for a leisurely weekend afternoon on the scenic grounds of royal tombs that surround the city. The tombs are set in fragrant pine forests and decorated with monumental stone sculptures. Popular tomb sites for a half-day's outing to the northeast of Seoul include Kŭmgok, Tonggu-nŭng and Kwang-nŭng. The best way to visit the tombs is by private car. To get to Kŭmgok, take the National Route 46 east; to Tonggu-nŭng, take National Route 46 to Kuri-si and turn north to T'oegyewŏn; to Kwang-nŭng, take National Route 47 from T'oegyewŏn. And take a picnic basket!

**POTTERY KILNS.** The former Yi Dynasty pottery-making village of Punwon-ni, near the town of Ich'ŏn, is a 1½-hour drive southeast of Seoul. Two important ingredients in making fine porcelain, good quality kaolin clay and firewood, were in abundance in this wooded area. Wares from the royal Punwon kilns were floated down the Han River to supply the palaces of Seoul. Today you can watch famous Seoul potters at work at their kilns and studios in Sukwang-ni and Sindung-myon, a few kilometers north of Ich'ŏn. Showrooms attached to their kilns sell wares at a fraction of the prices they command in Seoul. Another 30 minutes east of the Ich'ŏn kilns is Yoju, site of King Sejong's tomb and Silluk-sa Temple. Take National Road 3 to Ich'on and National Road 42 to Yoju.

**NO MAN'S LAND** is just an hour away from Seoul — the tense 4-kilometer wide demilitarized zone between North and South Korea. The zone has been largely given over to Nature since the Korean Armistice was signed in 1953, making for a wildlife reserve in what must be the most unusual location in the world. Most people visit Panmunjŏm, the village in the DMZ where the truce was signed, for a look at this relic of the Cold War. If you are fortunate, you may also see tall Manchurian cranes, a species of bird once thought to be extinct. There is one unsettling problem, however: the infrared scanners used by the United Nations Command soldiers to detect infiltrators cannot distinguish between a man and a large bird. This has resulted in many a

sleepless night for the GIs in the South who are never sure whether they will encounter a crane or a communist. Tours to Panmunjŏm, including lunch, can be arranged through the Korea Travel Bureau, (777-6647) or the USO, (795-3028).

**THE FOLK VILLAGE IN SUWŎN** is an enjoyable day-trip and introduction to Korean village life. Privately-owned and operated since 1973, the village has more than 230 faithful reconstructions of old houses from all parts of Korea. They range from simple peasant abodes to large aristocratic manors. Public squares for the performance of folk music and dance, studios for the demonstration of traditional crafts, and marketplaces for the sale of handicrafts and the sampling of country-style foods add excitement to the visit. Don't pass up the rustic taverns that serve *tongdong-ju*, a delicious rice wine. Tours of the village can be arranged through your hotel. Or take the #1 subway line to Suwŏn, then you can shuttle from Suwŏn station to the village by taxi or bus.

**HOT SPRINGS.** Two hours south of Seoul are the Onyang hot springs where Seoulites take the "waters" of the numerous *yŏgwans*, Korean inns, offering private rooms with piped-in mineral baths. Some establishments maintain additional communal pools with sauna and steamroom for W15,000–W25,000 per night. Massage and rub-down service is available at extra cost. The town is also famous for its fine Onyang Folk Museum, set in a spacious garden with a traditional foods snack bar. An antique shop sells nice pieces which did not make it into the museum's permanent collection. Take the Seoul–Pusan Expressway and exit east at Ch'ŏnan.

**HO'AM ART MUSEUM.** Opened to the public in 1981, this priceless collection of Korean art is the pride and joy of Lee Byung-chul, founder and chairman of the giant Samsung Group. The collection of more than 6,000 objects, including 12 designated as National Treasures, is only beginning to gain the recognition it deserves at home and abroad. Masterpieces from the collection are periodically displayed at the Ho'am Gallery in the Choong-ang Ilbo Building in downtown Seoul. But the museum itself is set on the slopes of a private mountain in Yongin which has been developed into a family-style park with amusement rides and safari animals. The park has several restaurants and snack bars. Take the Seoul–Pusan Expressway and, at Masong, get onto the Yongdong Expressway heading towards Kangnung.

**MIRŬK BUDDHA STATUES.** A pleasant half-day drive, including lunch, takes you to this site in P'aju-gun in the countryside north of Seoul. Drive along National Road 1 to Pyŏche and turn right at the railway line heading in the direction of Üijŏng-

bu on Route 39. After about two kilometers, turn left. When the road forks in the town, bear left. The two statues are visible from a distance on the right side of the road. Crudely carved out of the 17.4-meter rock in the 11th century, the two Buddhas registered as National Treasure #93, are folk images worshiped by women who desire children. The small statue on the shoulder of the Buddha on the left was added in 1953. A delicious *kalbi* or *pulgogi* barbecue can be enjoyed at one of the scenic outdoor restaurants along the way.

**HAN RIVER HALF-DAY TRIP.** Drive for an hour east along the Han River until you reach the confluence of its north and south branches. There you pass through beautiful unspoiled scenery along the banks. An hour's hike above the town of Yangsuri at the mouth of the North Han River is Sujong-sa, a temple built by King Sejo in 1458. The forested temple, which has bubbling springs and a beautiful stone pagoda added in 1493, is an ideal spot for a picnic. Drive on eastwards of Yangsuri for 40 minutes and you'll reach Yongmun-sa. This was erected during the reign of Queen Chindok (647–654) but has been rebuilt many times since. Its star attraction is a majestic 170-foot ginko tree, said to be the world's oldest and largest.

**KANGHWA-DO.** One hour east of Seoul, this is the third largest of Korea's many coastal islands. During the Mongol invasions of Korea in the 13th century and the incursions of the Manchus in the 17th century the island served as a place of refuge for the royal family. Places of interest include a large "northern-style" dolmen, the Ch'amsŏng-dan (Star-reaching Altar) on top of Mani-san Mountain for the worship of Tan'gun, the mythical founder of Korea, and two picturesque temples, the Chŏndŭng-sa and the Pomun-sa. The island is dotted with small farms, fishing villages and cottage industries serving Seoul. To get there take National Road 48 from Kimpo Airport.

**FORTUNE TELLING.** Modern living has not dissuaded Seoulites from consulting fortune tellers when faced with momentous decisions. At Mi'a-gogae (Mi'a-dong Pass) in Tonam-dong, northeast Seoul, is a district housing more than 50 fortune-telling shops. Many of the seers are blind. Others are purported to receive their powers from great Chinese classics such as the I-Ching or long meditation in Buddhist temples. Still others have Shamanistic backgrounds and speak through spirits. Sessions run W10,000. Get off the #4 subway line at the Sŏngshin Women's University station.

**TAEHAK-NO (COLLEGE STREET).** This is the place where the young and young-at-heart go to relax and absorb some culture. Paved with more than 40 cozy cafes, art galleries, and performance halls, the street is closed to vehicular traffic on most weekends and during special cultural events. The focus is the Marronnier Park Complex, home of the Munye Theater and the ultra-modern Fine Arts Center. Taehak-no is a good place to watch street theater and amateur performances. Take the #1 subway to Chong-no 5-ga or the #4 line to Hyehwa.

**PEOPLE WATCHING AT YŎ'IU-DO PLAZA.** This great expanse of concrete was formerly an airport cum air base. It's now used as an emergency landing strip as well as a site for huge religious and officially-sponsored political rallies. Seoulites, however, have made it into a "people's playground" and, on Sundays, thousands turn out to bicycle or skateboard. You can watch or rent a bike at the plaza and join in the fun. Ceramic makers and potters exhibit and sell their wares here at 30 to 40 per cent below retail prices in a Thieves Bazaar each October. Yŏ'ui-do has no subway service but can be reached by a short bus or taxi ride from downtown.

**TWICE-YEAR MUSEUM.** The Kansong Art Museum at 97-1 Songbuk-dong is only open for two weeks in May and October but that belies its importance in the world of Korean art. The museum houses what may be the finest private collection of Korean painting in the world, as well as Koryŏ celadons and early Buddhist art. The patriot Chon Hyong-pil started the collection in the 1930s, selling his family lands in order to keep Korea's art treasures out of the hands of wealthy Japanese. Call 762-0442.

**UNIVERSITY MUSEUMS.** Almost every university in Seoul has a collection of Korean art, usually in the campus library or its own museum. The displays are less formal than in government museums and allow for a more intimate enjoyment of the objects, some of which are registered National Treasures. Prominent university museums include: Ehwa Woman's University (ceramics and furniture), 362-6301, ext. 667; Korea University (painting), 942-644; Seoul National University (painting and archaeology), 877-5693; Dongguk University (Buddhist arts), 267-8131, ext. 3261; Sejong University (costumes, ceramics and furniture), 467-1701; Dankook University (costumes) 797-0581.

**SEOUL NORIMADANG.** Watch free performances of authentic Korean mask dances, farmer's dances, folk songs, percussion and *kayagum* music at this amphitheater at 47 Chamshil-dong, Kangdong-ku, on the western edge of Sŏkch'on Lake at Chamshil. Shows are scheduled throughout the year to celebrate festival days on the farmer's almanac. Audience instruction and participation are actively encouraged at many shows. Performances are listed in English newspapers. Get off at the Chamshil stop on the #2 subway line.

## Seoul Best Bets

**BIRD'S-EYE VIEW** is from the 63-Building, the 264-meter Daehan Life Insurance Building which has 60 floors above ground and three below, making it one of the tallest skyscrapers in Asia. The observation deck on the 60th floor commands a breathtaking panorama of Seoul. On a clear day, you can see as far as the Yellow Sea to the west and across the DMZ right to the rocky landscapes of North Korea. The building's other attractions include a 3-D cinema with a Dolby-stereo sound system, an aquarium teeming with talking mermaids and a row of deluxe restaurants on the 56th floor.

**COUNTRYWIDE GUIDES** are fairly numerous. The best include *Korea Guide* by Edward B. Adams and *Korea and Taiwan, A Travel Survival Kit* by Lonely Planet Publications. *Korea*, by Leonard Lueras and Nedra Chung, in the Insight Guides series is good but needs an update. The most scholarly and up-to-date history is *A New History of Korea* by Lee Ki-baik, the most readable Wanne J. Joe's *Traditional Korea: A Cultural History*. The most complete and reliable guide to Seoul's historical sites is *Discovering Seoul* by Donald N. Clark and James H. Grayson. The best directories to Seoul shopping, restaurants, sites and services are *Seoul City Guide* by Anh Graphics and *Inside Seoul* by Honam Oil. For those relocating to Seoul, Richard B. Rucci's *Living in Korea* combines an American perspective with practical advice.

**ANTIQUE FURNITURE.** Shop at Insa-dong or Mrs Go's Collection, 400-24 Sŏgyo-dong, Map'o-gu (Tel. 322-3169), for collector's pieces; and at Ko Mi Dang (see Mr Kok Han-sung), 737-4 Hannam-dong (795-2538), next to the New Yongsan Hotel for medium-quality pieces. Cheap pieces can be found at Hwa Sung Art Products (ask Mr Chung Bong-woong to show you his warehouse), 124-4, It'ae-wŏn (793-2225), and Cheong Yang Dang Antiques (Mr Kim Myong-hwan), #108 Woo Seong Building, 255-9 Chang-anp'yŏng (244-6120 and 447-8908).

**REPRODUCTION FURNITURE** of fine quality is available at Wha An Designs, 194-4 Hanaro Building basement, Insa-dong (735-2588). Medium-quality pieces are found at Tong-in Store, 16 Kwanhun-dong in Insa-dong (733-4827), while cheap pieces can be purchased in It'ae-wŏn or Gallery 69, 67-5 Taehyun-dong, near Ewha Woman's University (363-0325).

**JEWELRY** at Turtle Hong's (see Mr Hong Sung-duk) in the Dong-ho Plaza, 83-1 It'ae-wŏn (794-9690) is reasonably-priced. This store also does custom work and repairs. White jade, smoky topaz and amethyst are native stones and make good buys for friends and relatives back home.

**FINE ANTIQUE DEALERS** who speak good English are Mr Hahn Yong-koo, 145-24 Sŏngbuk-dong

(762-2365 and 732-3946) and Mrs Byun Kyung-sook, 194-4 Hanoro Building basement, Insa-dong (735-2588). Both will be happy to answer queries.

**ALL-NIGHT EATERIES AND CAFES** at Pangbae-dong, south of the Han River, catering to night owls, peak at 3 a.m. Prices are a little higher than downtown, but these joints are chic and you can go Korean, Chinese, Japanese or Western.

**THE ROYAL ASIATIC SOCIETY** offers the best selection of books on Korea and runs well-organized day and weekend trips to spots all over South Korea. Their free lectures twice monthly on all aspects of Korean life and culture draw a large audience of foreigners as well as Koreans. Address: #611 Christian Building, Chong-no 5-ga (763-9483).

**SEOUL BARBERSHOPS** aim not only to make men look better but also feel better. A W10,000 haircut outside hotels includes shampoo and conditioning, body massage and facial treatment, manicure and pedicure, ear-cleaning, and a gentle snooze at the end. The government periodically campaigns against "other services" offered at barbershops. If you prefer to avoid these "special" extras, stick to the barbers in the better hotels.

**HAIRDRESSERS** in the downtown area are Park Seoung Chol (755-6016), on the southern edge of Myŏng-dong opposite the Pacific Hotel, whose clientele includes famous movie stars and models, and Suji Beauty Parlor in the Lotte First Avenue Arcade beneath the hotel, which offers full body and facial massage (799-3702).

**NIGHT MARKETS** are in Myŏng-dong and the East Gate area between Ch'ŏnggyech'ŏn-no 4-ga and 6-ga. As dusk settles, carts and stalls appear offering everything imaginable to buy or eat.

**ACUPUNCTURE TREATMENTS** for all your aches and pains are available at the Hospital of Oriental Medicine, Hyunghee University, Hoigi-dong, Dongdaemun-ku (965-8000). Ask for Professor Kang Sung-keel. The hospital also offers a special therapy to help people quit smoking.

**HOME STAY** for those who wish to experience short visits with a typical Seoul family, contact the Private Home Stay advisor in the Tourist Information Center at City Hall Plaza (731-7161), or the Korea Tourist Bureau (KTB) — (585-1911).

**PUB** is Bobby London's on the basement level of the Lotte Hotel off City Hall Plaza. The popular buffet features roast beef and *sashimi*.

**WESTERN LUNCHEON BUFFET** can be got at the Oak Room in the Hilton Hotel on Namsan Mountain. It is popular with business people.

**DELICIOUS LUNCHEON SALADS** are available at the Peninsula Cafe in the Lotte Hotel near City Hall Plaza. Spinach and Nicoise salads are a big hit with calorie-conscious diners.

**JOURNALIST'S WATERING-HOLE** is the Ninth Gate Bar in the Westin Chosun Hotel near City Hall Plaza. Watch the twilight shadows dance on the Altar of Heaven erected by King Kojong in 1897.

**TAILOR** patronized by U.S. President Ronald Reagan is U.S. Kim Tailors in It'ae-wŏn. Korean executives often go to AQ Tailors, which has a branch in the Westin Chosun Hotel. But the majority opinion is that Seoul is not in the running to be Asia's top tailoring capital. Except for posh boutiques in Myŏng-dong and near the front gate of Ewha Woman's University, dressmaking is also disappointing and should be avoided.

**TOURIST MAP OF SEOUL** is the free government handout available at any branch of the Tourist Information Service. One branch is located behind City Hall, another at the Ch'ŏnggyech'ŏn-no and Namdaemun-no intersection.

**PERSONAL SEALS** are the legal equivalent of handwritten signatures in Korea. Get a *tojang* carved in wood (W500) or stone (W2,000) with your name in fancy Chinese characters to take home as a souvenir. The alleys behind the Kyobo Building and the U.S. Embassy in Kwanghwa-mun are dotted with *tojang* shops.

**HANDMADE PAPER** in a rainbow of colors for gift-wrapping or in plain white for oriental painting is an excellent buy at W200 per sheet. In earlier times, handmade Korean paper or *hanji* was much sought after by Chinese scholar-painters. Insa-dong carries the best selection in Seoul.

**LACQUERWARE BOXES** in plain black or red, or inlaid with mother-of-pearl, make attractive gifts. Avoid the cheap grades of inlaid lacquer where the inlays are of inferior quality and are set by machine. Several good shops are located on Namdaemun-no 4-ga near the Saerona Department Store off the South Gate Market area.

**HANDICRAFTS** can be found at the Korean Handicrafts Direct Sales Market, 21 Namdaemun-no near the South Gate, (753-9341/2), the Korea Folk Handicrafts Center at 130-17 Chamwon-dong, Kangnam-ku, northeast of the Express Bus Terminal (532-9161), and also at the Tong-in Store at 16 Insa-dong-gil (733-4827).

**HANDKNIT SWEATERS** in traditional Irish fisherman designs can be bought from Hallim Weavers (the wool comes from sheep ranches on Cheju-do), shop #26 in the Westin Chosun Hotel arcade. More fashionable handknits for the entire family in wool or acrylic can be purchased from Hyun Hee Handicraft Cooperative, which supports displaced Vietnamese wives and children of Korean veterans of the Vietnam War, in the basement of Yongdong Presbyterian Church, Chong-no 5-ga (763-7269). You'll need one in winter.

**KOREAN SILKS AND SATINS** are sold at the East Gate Market (look for the Chintz Building with the daisy emblem) or the Silk Fabrics Street behind the Pohin-gak (Bell Pavilion) on Chong-no 2-ga.

**MASSAGE AND SAUNA** for men and women is best at the Riverside Hotel, 341-1 Chamwon-dong, Kangnam-ku (543-1001). For men only, try the Shin Shin Hotel in the alley beside the Bank of Korea across from the Shinsaege Department Store, 93-43 Pukch'ang-dong (777-9331). This popular bathing place has long been in business and is open 24 hours a day. The truly adventurous must try bathing in an ordinary *mogyokt'ang*, or public bathhouse. Every neighborhood has one and it can be identified by the following symbol: ♨

**JAPANESE AND CHINESE FOOD.** Seoul chefs have no qualms about localizing the delicate cooking of Japan and the complex cuisine of China by dousing it with overdoses of garlic, chili peppers or other spices. Japanese food is most authentic in the deluxe hotels. Outside, Japanese residents of Seoul patronize the Manseon at 210 Hangang-no 2-ga, Yongsan-ku (797-2329) — in an alley beside the Kukje Center Building. Chinese residents find the restaurants in the deluxe hotels disappointing. Those who speak Mandarin call ahead to the Hyang-wŏn, 226-36 Yonnam-dong, Map'o-ku (323-3421) and order their meal from owner Yi Hyang-pang, who is a protege of Fu Pei-mei, the famous Taipei chef noted throughout Asia.

**FRENCH NOUVELLE CUISINE** is served at the Seasons in the Hilton Hotel on Namsan Mountain, or at L'abri, 2nd floor of the Kyobo Building at the Kwanghwa-mun intersection (739-8830/1).

**ITALIAN DINING** can be enjoyed at Il Ponte in the Hilton and at La Cantina in the basement of the Samsung Building (the building that has a Chase Manhattan Bank on the first floor, across from the Lotte Hotel), Ŭlchi-ro 1-ga, Chongno-ku (777-2579).

**TEMPURA EXTRAVAGANZA** is whipped up by *tempura* maestro Kim Suh-mun at Sunwon, 4th floor of the Seoulin Hotel near the T'aep'yŏng-no and Ch'ŏnggyech'ŏnno intersection downtown.

**MOVIE STAR'S HANGOUT** is the Monnizer owned by actress Kim Po-ae. This rustic drinking joint features hearty home brews served with traditional side dishes like *pindaettŏk* (bean-flour pancakes) and deep-fried sesame leaves. The clientele is a fluid mix of laborers who come in to fill their stomachs and the upper crust, who are simply slumming. Address: 747-2 Hannam-dong, at the eastern end of It'ae-wŏn (795-0394).

**CLASSICAL KOREAN MUSIC AND DANCE** at its most authentic are at the Sejong Cultural Center near Kwanghwa-mun (736-2721), the National Theater on Namsan Mountain (274-1153), and

Munye Theater on Taehak-no (762-5231). Call direct or check the English newspapers for scheduled performances.

**SPACE THEATER** is classroom-sized but offers intimate *avant garde* and traditional folk performances, sometimes of outstanding quality. It's located near the Secret Garden on Yulgok-no Street (763-0771). Take the number 3 subway line to Anguk Station.

**KOREA HOUSE** presents an evening of Korean royal court cuisine and music and dance provided by members of the National Classical Music and Dance Institute. Address: P'il-dong 2-ga, Chung-ku (266-9101). Call for the times and current prices.

**IT'AE-WŎN** is a tourist shopping street that seems to grow more fantastic and glittering by the month as the old stalls are replaced by modern shopping arcades. You can find some of the best bargains in Asia here. The quality of goods is steadily improving, English is widely-used, and U.S. dollars are openly accepted. There are excellent buys on furs, leather and suede jackets, eelskin handbags, suit-

cases and carryalls, silk dresses, athletic shoes, and casual clothing for the entire family.

**CLASSICAL KOREAN COOKING** is not based on rich sauces or a complex blend of flavorings and spices. Foods come either *au naturel* or smothered in garlic, chili peppers, soya sauce and sesame oil. It is an extreme cuisine for a people prone more to excess than moderation. The best places to try *hanjong-sik*, or full-course Korean dinners, are at Yong Soo San (732-3019) and Nam Moon (732-3423), both in Samch'ŏng-dong or the Yoon Jeong in P'yŏngch'ang-dong (353-5253). The Yoon Jeong, managed by actress Yoon Yo-jeong is an elegant new establishment located mid-slope on Samgak-san while the Yong Soo San and Nam Moon are well-established houses that are located in an atmospheric old Seoul neighborhood.

**DISCOS** are the Xanadu in the Westin Chosun Hotel and the Rainforest in the Hilton Hotel. For more local color, try the Sportsmen's Club, an old standby, or its three trendier upmarket competitors — Gatsby, Rumors, and Pashu, all in It'ae-wŏn.

## Travel Notes

### How to Get There

#### By Air

Air connections to Seoul are improving steadily, both in terms of frequency and routing. Direct flights between the capital and North American destinations are increasing, particularly on the national carrier, Korean Air, and there are some now available to Europe as well. Direct flights from Japan to Pusan and Cheju Island offer further possibilities of travel within Korea to or from Seoul.

#### By Train

Domestic rail service aboard comfortable express trains is available to all major cities in Korea. Tickets should be purchased well in advance.

#### By Boat

Ferries arrive at Pusan from the Japanese ports Shimonoseki and Osaka.

#### By Bus

An efficient and inexpensive network of express highway buses connects all major cities in the country. There are frequent departures from the Seoul Express Bus Terminal in Panp'o, conveniently-located south of the Han River.

### When to Go

Korea has four distinct seasons with sharp variations in temperature. The best times to visit Korea are in the spring and fall, when the weather can be delightful. In January, the mercury can plunge to −20°C when a windy cold front sweeps down from Siberia. This is followed by a warmer, more moist period, often accompanied by snowfall. Summers, on the other hand, are sweltering. The heat is sometimes broken by heavy rain from typhoons. From mid-June to mid-July, it is frequently overcast and rainy, although the timing and length of the rainy season varies from year to year.

### Airport

Kimpo International Airport is 17 kilometers from downtown Seoul and taxis are the most convenient means for getting to Seoul destinations from here. The fare for ordinary cabs is between W3,000 and W4,000, depending on the destination, and a listing of approximate cab fares is now posted outside the terminal. Ignore the touts inside the terminal who approach foreigners asking if a taxi is required and, instead, proceed out of the terminal, following the signs for the curbside taxi stand. If you have a lot of luggage, you may want to consider a tan "Call Taxi." These are more expensive but have larger trunks than the ordinary taxis. There is also an airport bus which runs every 20 minutes on a route through downtown Seoul. It costs W500.

### Bookshops

The oldest bookstore in Korea is Chongno Book Center on Chang-no 2-ka. Here you can find a good selection of books on Korea in English. Kyobo Book Center at Kyobo Building, and the Royal Asiatic Society at Chong-no 5-ka, also stock an extensive collection of books on Korea. Other main bookshops are Pan Korea Book Corporation, Pan-mun Book Company and Korea Overseas Publications which are all found within the same vicinity.

### Bus Services

You can get anywhere in Seoul by public bus. The fare is W130 by exact change or W120 by tokens purchased in advance at most bus stops. There is no map of the system, so you'll have to ask which bus to take. Be prepared to rub shoulders with Seoulites. There are also express buses, colored green or beige, that cost W350 and have guaranteed seats where you can rub elbows instead.

### Car Hire

The car rental business is growing rapidly, with self-drive daily rates starting from about W30,000 for small cars. Chauffeur-driven cars start from about W50,000 for ten hours, although shorter hire periods can be arranged as well. One-way rentals are not yet available. You can sometimes get a car rental brochure at the airport, or you could check with any major hotel. The old standby Hertz can be reached at Tel. 798-0801.

### Clothing

For business, Koreans are formal and suits are a must. Otherwise clothing needs to vary with the season, although Koreans are modest dressers and always keep themselves well covered up.

### Communications

Korea has been continuously improving its telephone service, and both domestic and international services are usually excellent, with IDD available in most parts of the city and at all major hotels. Public phone booths take two ten-*wŏn* coins, but will cut off the call after about three minutes regardless of the number of coins that have been stuffed in. Depending on where the call is going to, language can be a problem and, if you are calling a local organization, help from a Korean-speaker could be useful, if not a necessity.

Public telex is available beside the Central Post Office on Namdaemunno 2ga, and at the Korea Telecommunication Authority Building between the U.S. Embassy and the Kyobo Building. Major hotels offer telex and facsimile services and will often send outgoing messages for non-hotel guests.

The domestic mail service is good, however, the international service often seems unnecessarily delayed, although international express mail services are available. The courier service DHL (Tel. 77134) will undertake deliveries to anywhere in the world.

## Customs

Passing through the Korean customs is an unpredictable experience; bags are invariably opened and inspected. Most travelers will experience no difficulties although some items, such as jewelry, video cameras and tape recorders, expensive cameras, or computers are dutiable if not re-exported within six months. Customs officers place a stamp in the passport; this is cancelled when the item is taken out of the country, and since the inspection point comes after the airline check-in counter, the item should not be checked in as baggage.

## Driving

Most short-term visitors have little reason to drive in the city, since public transportation is adequate; the road system is difficult to navigate and parking hard to find. Koreans are aggressive drivers, and the accident rate is high. A traffic accident resulting in bodily injury can land everyone in jail until the situation is clarified. If these points do not scare you off, all you need is a valid international driver's permit, and lots of guts.

Driving to get out of the city and see the countryside is a more attractive proposition, but extreme caution and defensive driving techniques are advised.

## Electricity

Electricity is generally supplied at 220 volts, and transformed down to 110. It is best to double check before you destroy your portable hair dryer.

## Health and Medical Care

Public health problems in Seoul are well under control. During the hot summer months one should exercise more than the usual caution about restaurant sanitation. During the months without the letter "r" — May, June, July and August — it is best to avoid raw seafood.

Should you need medical attention, hotels usually have doctors. The International Clinic at Severance Hospital (392-3404) has a small staff of foreign doctors, who will provide references to specialists on the hospital's staff when needed and help with the language problem. There is also FOCUS, the Foreigner's Community Service organization, which can provide the names of doctors who speak foreign languages: call 798-7529, or 765-0859, or 797-7121 ext. 280 after 4 p.m. Korean doctors are generally quite competent despite the primitive appearance of the surroundings in which they work.

## Hotels

The standards of hotel services have steadily improved with the opening of each new luxury class hotel. While fairly comfortable, they are still not up to the high standards set in other Asian cities like Bangkok, Hong Kong or Singapore. The hotels aim to serve, but their notions of service are often quite rigid and there can be lapses, as in message-taking, that often result from the language problem.

The following is a list of the various classes of hotels available:

**Luxury Class**
— Seoul Hilton, near Namdae-mun (753-7788).
— Hyatt Regency, Namsan/It'ae-wŏn (798-0061).
— Lotte, near City Hall (77110).
— Sheraton Walker Hill, in the eastern suburbs of the city (444-8211).
— Shilla, near Namsan and the National Theater in the city center (233-3131).
— Westin Chosun, City Hall area (77105).

**First Class**
— Ambassador, near Namsan and the National Theatre (275-1101).
— King Sejong, near Myŏng-dong (776-1811).
— Koreana Hotel, near City Hall and Kwanghwa-mun (720-991).
— Pacific Hotel, Namsan (777-7811).
— Plaza Hotel, next to City Hall Plaza (77122).
— Hotel President, City Hall Plaza (753-3131).
— Ramada Olympia Hotel, north of the city center (353-5131).
— Seoul Royal, Myŏng-dong (77145).
— Seoulin Hotel, off Kwanghwa-mun (732-0181).
— Tower Hotel, Namsan (253-9181).

**Economy**
— Crown Hotel, It'ae-wŏn (792-8224).
— Hamilton Hotel, It'ae-wŏn (794-0171).
— Mammoth Hotel, Ch'ŏngyang-ni, west of the city center on the number 1 subway line (965-5611).
— Savoy Hotel, Myŏng-dong (776-2641).
— Seoul Hotel, near Kwanghwa-mun (722-0181).
— YMCA Hotel, on Chong-no — the cheapest of the registered hotels (722-8291).

## Language

Korean belongs to the Ural-Altaic family of languages. Its grammatical structure is similar to Japanese, with about half the vocabulary derived from Chinese. It is one of the world's most difficult languages to learn. Older Koreans often speak Japanese. English is studied by the younger generation, although the achievements are often disappointing and communication in hotels or taxis is sometimes a problem. When translating prices into English, Koreans frequently mistakenly transpose

decimal points, with some amazing results; if there is any confusion about prices, write them down.

## Mass Media

The local English newspapers have an extensive coverage of domestic news, but they are rather dull, and inadequate when it comes to reporting on the happenings around the world; on the other hand, the *Asian Wall Street Journal* and the *International Herald Tribune* may be unpredictably delayed for several days. Thus, if you like to stay abreast of the international scene, a shortwave radio is helpful. You can also tune in to the American Armed Forces Network broadcasts for American network news, and can be forgiven for thinking you're in a Chicago hotel room when you catch the World Series and the Superbowl live!

## Money Matters

The Korean *wŏn* is not subdivided. As of 1987, the exchange rate hovered at about W830 to one U.S. dollar, and the *wŏn* is expected to appreciate. Coins are available in one, five, ten, 50, 100 and 500 *wŏn* denominations, while there are 1,000, 5,000 and 10,000 *wŏn* notes.

Any amount of cash or its equivalent may be imported, but must be declared if in excess of US$5,000. Money may be exchanged at the airport at standard bank rates. Hotels will also exchange cash or travelers checks for an added commission. Exchange receipts should be saved for reconversion upon leaving the country.

International credit cards are accepted at major hotels, stores and an increasing number of restaurants. There are, however, some establishments which accept only credit cards issued in Korea. It is best to check in advance if in doubt.

## Museums and Palaces

The National Central Museum, housing the largest and finest collection of Korean art in the world, has been relocated in the old Japanese-built Capitol Building. It is entered through the open gates of the Kwanghwa-mun.

Behind the Museum is the Kyŏngbok-kung, the royal palace of the Yi Dynasty. Within the palace complex is the National Folklore Museum.

The Ch'angdŏk-kung, the best preserved of the Yi Dynasty palaces, and the Piwon (Secret Gardens) behind it can be seen by group tours that leave from the front gate of the complex between 9 a.m. and 5 p.m. At present English tours start at 10:30 a.m., 12:30 p.m. and 2:30 p.m. while Japanese tours start at 11:30 in the morning, and 1:30 and 3:30 in the afternoon.

The National Museum of Modern Art is located south of the city as part of the Seoul Grand Park complex near Kwach'ŏn. The museum is housed in a spectacular new building that is perhaps more impressive than the collection within.

## Tours

The hotel desks can provide brochures on the more common tours available. These organized tours are recommended for trips out of the city which are difficult or costly for the lone traveler. Do-it-yourself tours are easy to plan and execute within the city and its immediate environs.

## Taboos and Customs

Koreans have their own way of doing things, and they are resistant to change. They can be quite rude to strangers on the street, while delightfully polite to anyone with a proper introduction. You are not likely to offend anyone if you try to be polite, restrained and conservative.

Shoes should always be removed before entering a house or temple. If you visit a home, take a token gift of fruit or flowers. Do not smoke or cross your legs in front of your elders. Remember, Koreans are embarrassed by public displays of affection and regard uncovered flesh with disfavor, but they do make allowances for Westerners.

For doing business, always have a name card, and hand it over with the right hand. You might want to study the card you receive, as yours will certainly be scrutinized. (Yes, indulge yourself and stick those extra titles on your card, they make all the difference.) Koreans do not split bills; the one who does the inviting pays. Finally, Korean men generally do not have much respect for women of any race, but will swallow their prejudices and treat foreign professional women more or less as such.

## Taxis

Taxi drivers in Seoul seem to be a law unto themselves. At most times, taxis are not difficult to find. During rush hour, late in the evening, or during the late afternoon shift changes, however, they seem to disappear. They may refuse to go to some destinations and often cruise the downtown areas. The etiquette calls for the prospective passenger to shout in Korean the destination and hope the driver stops. This often works. Drivers of ordinary taxis almost never try to cheat their fares; they are more interested in getting to the destination and finding another passenger.

The tan-colored "Call Taxis" are more expensive, but they often appear just as you have given up hope of ever getting a taxi at all. Occasionally drivers may try to charge a fixed fare off the meter. This is illegal and, unless you are desperate for the ride, you should refuse and report the driver to the tourism authorities.

## Theft and Crime

Violent crimes against foreigners are almost unheard of, and you can walk safely through the city. In crowded markets or on buses, however, watch your wallet or purse. If your wallet is snatched, it will most likely turn up a few days later at the police station with only cash missing. You should, therefore, keep something in your wallet that will help the police to locate you.

## Time

Seoul is nine hours ahead of GMT, the same as Tokyo. In 1987, Korea began to set the clocks one hour forward during the summer.

## Photography

The Korean authorities are sensitive about some kinds of photographs for security reasons (never forget, South Korea is technically a nation at war), but this should not affect you unduly. The list of prohibited subjects includes military facilities, overviews of the city, harbors, airports, underground shopping areas, crosswalks and certain buildings—impossible to know which ones. There are so many plainclothesmen around that you are hardly likely to have time to click the shutter before being stopped. It is best to be cooperative.

## Police

It is hard to turn around in Seoul without bumping into the police. Some have blue uniforms; some, the traffic police, have green uniforms; while others, the riot police, wear khaki. Many have no uniforms at all and do not carry any identification. (They are nonetheless easily recognized by their crew cuts and, depending on the season, their ill-cut suits, sneakers, jeans and sports jackets, or long tan coats. They appear to be loitering and often have what looks like a hearing aid in one ear.) The police generally leave foreigners alone, but you should cooperate with them to avoid trouble. If you have an Asian face, be sure to have your passport at all times or you run the risk of being picked up as a suspected North Korean spy. If you go to the police with a problem, they are usually very helpful and polite although almost none of them speak any foreign languages. The police emergency number is 112, but have a Korean speaker place the call.

## Public Holidays

**January 1–3**
The New Year is celebrated as a 3-day holiday. Many Seoulites return to their country homes.
**Late January or early February**
The Lunar New Year was revived as a national holiday in 1985. The Japanese had ended the celebration of the traditional New Year and substi-

tuted it with the Western New Year. This holiday is now called Folk Holiday.
**March 1**
Independence Day celebrates the 1919 uprising against Japanese colonial rule.
**April 5**
Arbor Day. South Korea is the only developing country in the world to have successfully reforested its once bare mountains.
**Early May**
The 8th day of the 4th lunar month is one of Korea's most colorful holidays. There is a huge lantern procession through downtown Seoul and thousands of multihued lanterns are hung in all the temples throughout the country. This is a good opportunity to catch Koreans going out in traditional dress on a warm spring day.
**May 5**
Children's Day.
**August 15**
Liberation Day celebrates the end of Japanese colonial rule.
**Late September or early October**
The 15th day of the 8th lunar month is *Ch'usŏk*, the harvest moon festival, the most important of the folk holidays of South Korea.
**October 1**
Armed Forces Day.
**October 3**
Foundation Day celebrates the mythical founding of the nation by Tan'gun in 2333 BC.
**October 9**
Han'gŭl Day celebrates the invention of the Korean writing system, supervised by King Sejong in the 15th century. The system is surprisingly logical and easy to learn.
**December 25**
Christmas is growing in importance as more of the population converts to Christianity.

## Tipping

The general rule is don't tip. Most hotels have a "no tipping" policy and instead charge 10% service. Taxi drivers do not expect anything unless they help with the luggage or perform some unusual service. You might leave a tip at Western restaurants outside the hotels if they do not charge for service.

## Toilets

Parks and other public facilities have public toilets, sometimes of the "squat" variety, although Western toilets are becoming more common. Nearly all restaurants have their own toilets, as do shopping arcades in major buildings. Between these and the many hotels sprinkled around the city, finding a public toilet is never a problem.

## Tourist Information

The Seoul City government has set up tourist information booths all around the city to help travelers, largely in anticipation of the influx of foreign visitors expected to come with the 1988 Olympic Games. Unfortunately they are not always manned. They have forms for complaints and you can rest assured that they will follow up on them. A tourist information center has been opened in the basement of the Korean National Tourism Building at the intersection of Namdaemun-no and Ch'ŏnggyech'ŏn-no (Tel. 757-0086). There is also an information/complaint center (Tel. 724-4034) adjacent to the City Hall, where you can get free maps.

## Visas

A 15-day transit visa is now available upon arrival for short-term travel in South Korea, so long as you can show a confirmed onward travel booking. A tourist visa is easily obtained abroad and it allows stays for up to 60 days. Nationals of some countries are exempted from visa requirements according to bilateral agreements, and a call to the local Korean consulate can confirm this. There are other special purpose short-term visas which are easily obtained. A resident visa can take many weeks to process and applications should be made months in advance of the expected date of travel.

Be sure to enter Korea with a proper visa to avoid difficulties at immigration. Visa types cannot be changed when you are in the country, so do not enter on a tourist visa and expect to be able to convert this to a work visa.

## Subways

Seoul has an extensive subway system that is useful for traveling from the downtown to many of the outlying areas. Important and frequently traveled areas, such as It'ae-won or Yŏ'ui-do are unfortunately not on the grid, but the trains do go to the Olympic Park south of the river.

## Water

Some foreigners in Seoul drink the water from the tap and claim to have no difficulties. Most drink bottled water, which is easily available. The problem with the city water supply seems not so much to be bacterial contamination as heavy metal pollution.

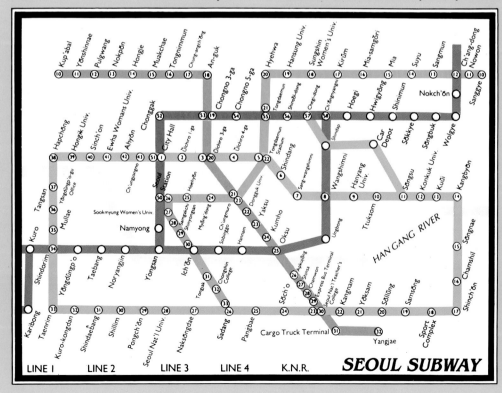

SEOUL SUBWAY

LINE 1    LINE 2    LINE 3    LINE 4    K.N.R.

# Index

***Buddhism claims** the largest following in South Korea. At Pŏngwon-sa Temple, ferocious gods and warriors (**above and left**) and the dragon and phoenix (**overleaf**), freshly-painted in symbolic religious colors, festoon the buildings. An enterprising merchant sells curios and used gear salvaged from old ships along It'ae-wŏn's main shopping thoroughfare (**preceding page**).*